S.K.I.T.

A Three-Part Series of Practical and Non-Judgmental Lesson Plans to Support Kids in Transition

by
Irene Clouse Newlon

Support for Kids in Transition (S.K.I.T.)

Copyright © 1996 by Irene Clouse Newlon

Published by KIDSRIGHTS®, an imprint of JIST Life, LLC,
a division of JIST Publishing, Inc.
8902 Otis Avenue
Indianapolis, IN 46216-1033
Phone: 1-800-892-5437   Toll-Free Fax: 1-877-543-7001   E-mail: kreditorial@jist.com

Visit our Web site at www.kidsrights.com for our online catalog, information on
KIDSRIGHTS, free information on social issues today, and author biographies!

Quantity discounts are available for KIDSRIGHTS books.
Please call our Client Services Department at 800-892-5437
for a free catalog and more information.

Printed in the United States of America

05 04 03 02 01   9 8 7 6 5

ISBN: 1-55864-040-1

Order Code: K1508

Table of Contents

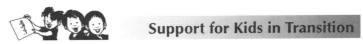

WELCOME TO THE S.K.I.T. PROGRAM!

We hope that you will be able to use the information and lesson plans to create or improve children's support group programming within your agency.

HOW DID S.K.I.T. BEGIN?

Support for Kids in Transition (S.K.I.T.) was developed from another similar program, Helping Kids Cope, which is currently being used by nonprofit organizations throughout the United States. Some of the programs that have incorporated HKC include spouse abuse shelters, day care centers and day camps for low-income families, support groups for children of incarcerated parents (SKIP), and runaway and homeless youth facilities. Children of all ages and from all types of housing and family situations have benefitted by participating in these support groups, specifically designed to address issues that affect them.

All of the forms and lesson plans have been tested, revised, and re-evaluated periodically to ensure that they **work**! For the most part, children who have participated in these sessions have enjoyed the experience.

HOW IS THE S.K.I.T. PROGRAM MANUAL ORGANIZED?

This Manual is designed to be a **working tool**, to help you implement the program with very little effort. It is also designed to be used by **volunteers**, one of your most valuable professional resources. Provided that the supplies and materials are available, a volunteer can read through and prepare for a lesson plan 30 minutes prior to each session.

Each lesson plan is **independent** of the others. They **are not** developmental in approach. Each session has closure, which is important when offering programming for children who are in temporary living situations. Remember, a child may be able to attend only one session.

Each session addresses one of the **four impact elements:**

1. Self-Esteem
2. Decision-Making Skills
3. Family and Friends
4. Substance Abuse (optional)

The manual is **general** in nature. It is not specific. You may use what you want and need for your program. Although there are numbers assigned to session plans to establish a continuity in the materials, there is no definite order in which they must be presented.

Because you may have children attend more than one session, it is suggested that a different impact element be presented for each of four sessions, then repeated.

The session plans are **flexible**. If you wish to take two session plans and present them at the same time to create a longer session, you can. If you choose to present two Self Concept sessions, one after the other, you can. If you do not wish to include substance abuse sessions in your group, you can. It is suggested that, at a minimum, each age group meet once per week and that each session last at least 1 hour, but no longer than 2 hours. All session plans are prepared to last approximately 1 to 2 hours.

There are enough session plans in each age group to continue for eight weeks without repetition. It is important to comment, at this time, that smaller children generally **love** repetition. It will not be detrimental to repeat sessions if a child will be in the program longer than eight weeks. It is also possible to intermix session plans to create new ones.

THE POINT IS, IT'S YOURS TO USE AS YOU WISH.

WHAT ABOUT THE PROGRAM FORMS?

Program forms included in this Manual are

1. Children's Intake- This can be completed for all children who participate and includes the parental permission statement. It can be helpful in gaining information about the family unit, providing information to the session facilitator, and collecting data for permanent funding.

2. Session Evaluation- This can be completed by the facilitator and will briefly explain each child's participation in the session. It is useful to facilitators and program managers and can offer insight into a child's behavior patterns.

3. Program Evaluation- This form can be completed by the facilitator and the parent(s) to gain valuable information about the effectiveness of the program and noticeable changes in a child's behavior.

ACTION STEPS

1. Review the Manual carefully.

2. Develop a Plan of Action and Time Frame for Implementation.

3. Develop a Staffing and Fund-raising Plan.

4. Compile a list of needed materials and supplies, and don't forget to include a room or place for sessions. (There has never been a *S.K.I.T.* program that did not have **everything** needed and more, after a list was distributed to churches and organizations.)

5. Let the public know what you are going to do. **Publicity!**

6. Provide *S.K.I.T.* training for facilitators.

7. BEGIN!

WHAT ARE FACILITATORS?

Facilitators are adults (or in some cases young adults, ages 15–21 years) who organize the lesson plans and activities for a particular session/age group. They are also the ones who actually "facilitate" the group and help to "guide" the children during the sessions. They are **not** there to perform therapy or to become the saviors of the children with whom they come in contact.

If your agency has a staff person(s) educated in social work/psychology who will be coordinating the *S.K.I.T.* program, it is important to know that these support sessions were developed on the most part by therapists. They are not therapy sessions, but therapeutic in nature.

If your agency will be recruiting volunteers as facilitators, make sure that they understand that some children may be able to attend only one session. An effective facilitator must not become too attached to the children themselves, but must become very attached to the **atmosphere** that they will be responsible for **creating**.

WHAT ABOUT SELECTING A S.K.I.T. STAFF?

It is very important that potential facilitators be screened and interviewed **prior** to their participation in a *S.K.I.T.* training program, and as facilitators in any *S.K.I.T.* session. There should always be a probationary period, just as with paid staff, so that if someone is not effective as a facilitator, he/she can be assigned to another more appropriate position or dismissed.

Remember, these sessions are for the children and the atmosphere is the key to the success of the program.

WHAT ABOUT TRAINING
S.K.I.T. STAFF?

It is **essential** that **all** facilitators participate in a *S.K.I.T.* training program prior to their placement. *The most important factor to stress during training is consistency. Children who are in temporary housing need this component more than others. It is like an old blanket or teddy bear; they can count on S.K.I.T. being there while they are in a temporary facility.*

Potential facilitators must be able to **commit** to attending **all** training sessions and *S.K.I.T.* sessions. They should also commit to a length of time (6 months to a year) so that your agency can depend on their services without leaving the *S.K.I.T.* sessions stranded. Many agencies establish a professionally written **contract** that *S.K.I.T.* volunteers/staff sign.

WHAT ABOUT DISCIPLINE?

During most sessions, the group will itself be performing the disciplinary role by continually reminding others about the **group rules** that are discussed and posted at the beginning of each session. If, however, there is a major disruption by a child or children, the following techniques can be helpful:

1. The first alternative is to offer the child a **"time out"** period. This usually can be done in some part of the room where the session is being held, but if the behavior continues or is serious enough, remove the child or children (one at a time) from the room. (Another good reason for co-facilitated groups.)

2. Second option, use Choice Behavior as follows:

   _____, you are screaming while the other children are trying to listen to
   name
   the story.

   You have a choice: You can stop screaming so that you and the others can hear the story, or you can leave the group for this session and try again at the next session if you are still here.

   Whatever **you** decide is fine and **I respect** your decision. (The key words in this sentence are **you** and **I respect**.)

Staff/Volunteer Training sessions should include more extensive information and skill building on this topic.

WHAT IS SPECIAL ABOUT S.K.I.T.?

Although *S.K.I.T.* is not therapy, lesson plans and activities offer a "therapeutic and support-oriented" environment for children who are in transition. Examples of transition are **homelessness, divorce, substance abuse, unemployment, new surroundings,** or any other situation that creates an unstable environment for the child.

Specific group rules have been developed and are incorporated into each session. The children may add their own rules, if all in the group, including the facilitator, are in agreement.

All activities are non-competitive, encourage cooperation, offer support and praise, and allow children the opportunity to express their feelings and opinions in a non-threatening environment. These opportunities are important to children, especially when they must live with many other families in a communal setting or feel that their atmosphere is unstable.

The most important element of each session is the positive daily message. Each meeting ends with this interaction so that children will leave with a good feeling about themselves.

S N A C K S

The carefully chosen items on the
Snack Time menu are a very
important element to incorporate
into sessions, because nutrition
affects a child's well-being.
Many of the children (and
their parents) have little or
no knowledge of healthy
foods and balanced meals,
and Healthy Snack Time is
an opportunity to present
and reinforce these concepts in
a fun way. It also allows time for
the children to relax and enjoy a
bit of social time.

A NOTE ABOUT SUBSTANCE ABUSE SESSIONS

These are optional lesson plans. There are many different viewpoints about the methodology of presenting substance abuse education. All *S.K.I.T.* lesson plans are designed as teaching models and an effort is made to ensure that each is non-judgmental in respect to the use of alcohol or drugs. They have been approved by many professionals who work directly with clients and families dealing with substance abuse issues. Because the incidence of substance abuse is often the cause of unstable environments, these lesson plans are considered an important part of the *S.K.I.T.* program.

Lessons are not developmental, therefore if a child has to miss a sessions, he/she will not feel uncomfortable when returning. Each lesson has closure so that if a child can come for only one or two sessions, he/she learns something. This is what makes *S.K.I.T.* an excellent program for families in transition.

In the past, the predecessors of the *S.K.I.T.* program (Helping Kids Cope and Support for Kids of Incarcerated Parents) have chosen to include parent(s) in one of the sessions or all sessions. *S.K.I.T.* allows time for children to be children in a children's environment and was never intended to be a tool to teach parenting skills. It is strongly recommended that, to the extent possible, parenting skills classes/groups be offered at the same time that children support groups are offered. Parental participation during *S.K.I.T.* sessions is most effective in conjunction with a parenting program such as *P.S. I Love You,* which is the companion to *S.K.I.T.* It is important that parents understand this philosophy up front.

HOW ARE CHILDREN ASSIGNED TO SESSIONS?

The program is designed to separate children by age and grade in order to group ability levels together. It is important to recognize that, because of the differences in emotional and developmental maturity of children, it may be necessary to "place" some children in a group that does not reflect their grade/age.

Through past experience, it has also been noted that some 3-year-olds are able to participate in *S.K.I.T.* lessons for preschool and some are not ready for the level of the activities presented. Because of this, the intake procedure also becomes a tool to decide placement. Observing and talking with children before they are given the opportunity to participate reduces the incidence of having to remove or change a child's group assignment. This can create hurt feelings, a sense of rejection, and sometimes tantrums. **Do not set the child up for failure.**

Parents must also be aware that they need to be available during the sessions, in case the child needs to leave because of discipline issues, illness, or other problems that might occur. *S.K.I.T.* IS NOT A BABYSITTING SERVICE.

S.K.I.T. INTAKE FORM

To be completed by parent

Child's Name: _____

Parent(s) Name: _____

Marital Status: Single   Married   (circle one)

Child's Siblings and Ages: _____

_____

_____

_____

(If more, list on the back)

School Grade: _____ (if summer, grade child will be in next year)

Has he/she been placed in special classes in school?   yes   no   (circle one)

If yes, what is the class? _____

What is this child's favorite hobby or activity? _____

_____

Do you have any problems disciplining this child?   yes   no   (circle one)

Chemical Dependency History (optional question):

Who: _____
is currently ( ) practicing drug/alcohol use   ( ) in treatment or recovering

I GIVE PERMISSION FOR MY CHILD/CHILDREN TO ATTEND THE *S.K.I.T.* PROGRAM. I WILL MAKE EVERY EFFORT TO ENSURE THAT THE ABOVE NAMED CHILD IS ABLE TO ATTEND THE SESSIONS. I WILL ALSO MAKE EVERY EFFORT TO PARTICIPATE IN A DESIGNATED GROUP SESSION IF I AM ASKED.

   PARENT'S SIGNATURE: _____

   DATE: _____

I am interested in attending parenting skills groups: yes   no   (circle one)

S.K.I.T. ASSIGNMENT SHEET

Parent Copy

Child's Name: _____

Group Session Time: _____

Group Session Dates:

           1st: _____

           2nd: _____

           3rd: _____

           4th: _____

Session Facilitator's Name: _____

MAKE SURE THAT YOU HAVE RECEIVED A COPY OF THE INTRODUCTION TO *S.K.I.T.* SO THAT YOU UNDERSTAND THE PROGRAM.

S.K.I.T. SESSION EVALUATION SHEET

To be completed by Session Facilitator

Child's Name: _____

Group Session Assignment Dates: 1st _____   2nd _____
                                  3rd _____   4th _____
(If the child attends more than 4 sessions, begin a new page.)

1st Session: ❏ Self Concept   ❏ Decision Making
                  ❏ Family/Friends   ❏ Substance Abuse

Date: _____

_____
_____
_____

2nd Session: ❏ Self Concept   ❏ Decision Making
                  ❏ Family/Friends   ❏ Substance Abuse

Date: _____

_____
_____
_____

3rd Session: ❏ Self Concept   ❏ Decision Making
                  ❏ Family/Friends   ❏ Substance Abuse

Date: _____

_____
_____
_____

4th Session: ❏ Self Concept   ❏ Decision Making
                  ❏ Family/Friends   ❏ Substance Abuse

Date: _____

_____
_____
_____

General Concerns/Comments: _____

POSITIVE DAILY MESSAGE

FACILITATOR SAYS:

YOU ARE A
SMART
FUN
CARING
PERSON

CHILD REPLIES:

YES, I AM!!

IF YOU DON'T FEEL LIKE YOU ARE,

FAKE IT UNTIL YOU MAKE IT!

S.K.I.T. GROUP RULES

EVERYONE GETS A TURN TO SPEAK.

YOU CAN PASS YOUR TURN.

NO PUT-DOWNS.

EVERYONE HAS EQUAL TIME TO SPEAK.

Additional rules may be added
if all of the group approves.

S.K.I.T. SNACK LIST

GENERAL SUPPLIES
Napkins, spoons, 3- or 5-oz. paper cups

AGE 3–6 YEARS

Activity 1   Several flavors of granola bars
Several types of juice (pineapple, orange, cranberry)

Activity 2   Fruit chewies (real fruit snacks)
Lemonade

Activity 3   Popcorn (prepared in an
air popper)
Water

Activity 4   Peanut butter
Assorted crackers
Apple juice (100%)

Activity 5   Nuts (pecans, almonds, walnuts, cashews)
Tang orange drink

Activity 6   Apple slices
Yogurt—3 flavors
Water, lemons

Activity 7   String cheese or other types of cheese
Juice (100%), juice drink (10%)

Activity 8   Sliced carrots, celery, cucumbers
Ranch-style dip
Juice (100%)

S.K.I.T. SNACK LIST (cont'd)

AGES 6–9 YEARS

Activity 1   Bagel chips or mini bagels
Cream cheese with strawberries or pineapple
Water or milk

Activity 2   String cheese or different types of cheese
(sharp cheddar, Monterey Jack, etc.)
Cranberry juice

Activity 3   Yogurt—chocolate, vanilla
Shortbread cookies
Juice (100%)

Activity 4   Italian bread sticks/melba toast
Cream cheese spread
Juice (100% & 10%)

Activity 5   Several flavors of granola bars
(oat, chocolate chip)
Several types of juice (pineapple,
orange, cranberry)

Activity 6   Wheat crackers
Peanut butter
Juice (100%)

Activity 7   Pre-sliced/cut fruit pieces such as cherries, pineapple, peaches, etc.
Shredded coconut, almonds or other nuts
Vanilla yogurt with splash of cherry juice
Water

Activity 8   Different flavors of rice cakes
Juice (100%)

S.K.I.T. SNACK LIST (cont'd)

<u>AGES 9–12 YEARS</u>

Activity 1   Pre-sliced/cut fruit (cherries, pineapple, peaches, apples)
Shredded coconut
Almonds or other nuts
Vanilla yogurt with a splash of cherry juice
Paper cups and spoons
Water

Activity 2   Cereal (Cheerios, Apple Jacks, Fruit Loops)
Dried fruit, fruit roll-up pieces
Yarn
Milk or water

Activity 3   Rice cakes (plain)
Peanut butter
Juice (100%) (3 flavors)

Activity 4   Frozen yogurt
Squeezable cake decorator frosting
Water
Paper plates

Activity 5   Granola bars, several flavors
Juice (100%)

Activity 6   American, Swiss, and cheddar cheese slices
Crackers
Water or juice (100%)

Activity 7   Vegetables (carrots, celery, broccoli)
Ranch-style dip
Juice (100%) or water

Activity 8   English muffins or mini bagels
Cream cheese (flavored with pineapple, strawberries)
Juice (100%)

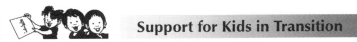

NOTES:

AGES 3 THRU 6

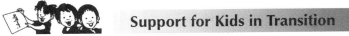

ACTIVITY 1
SELF-ESTEEM

BEFORE THE SESSION

Materials:

- Plastic name tag covers
- Index cards or stiff paper cut to fit size of tag
- Glue and glitter
- 4-foot pieces of white butcher paper, one for each child
- Crayons and markers
- Pencils
- Material scraps, ric-rac, lace, felt, yarn
- Hand mirror(s)
- Tape or thumbtacks
- Scissors

HELLO
What I Like To Do Best
(5 minutes)

Facilitator: Introduce yourself and the *S.K.I.T.* program. Discuss the rules for being a part of the group. (Refer to Poster or Rules page.)

Have everyone sit in a circle at the table or on the floor. Each child is to say his/her name the first time around. The second time around, the child is to say (in sentence form) "my name is _____, and one of the things I like to do best is _____." (Facilitator can start with his/her comment if the group is shy.)

Example: My name is Linda, and one of the things I like to do best is read books.

REMEMBER TO REINFORCE THE POSITIVE DAILY MESSAGE WITH EACH CHILD SOMETIME DURING THE SESSION.

"YOU ARE A SMART, FUN, CARING PERSON!"
"YES, I AM!"
"IF YOU DON'T FEEL LIKE YOU ARE, FAKE IT 'TIL YOU MAKE IT!"

GAME/ EXERCISE ACTIVITY
(10 minutes)

Name Tags

Directions: On pre-cut index cards, have children print their first name in large letters and decorate with markers, or print their name on the index card for them. Children can go over the letters with glue and glitter.

Put the name card into the plastic name tag cover and have the children clip on their shirts (help those who are small). Name tags should be removed from the plastic cover at the end of the session for future use but children may keep the name card.

S.K.I.T. LEARNING ACTIVITY
(35–40 minutes)

Me, Myself, and I

Goal: To help children identify their physical characteristics and feel good about those characteristics.

Directions: Divide the children into partners (preferably with another child they do not know very well). If there is an odd number, form a threesome.

1. Give two large sheets of butcher paper, markers, scissors, felt, and other materials to each pair of children.

S. K. I. T.
LEARNING   *(cont'd)*
ACTIVITY

---

2. Instruct children that they will take turns lying down on their back on the large white paper while their partner draws an outline around the edge of the body onto the paper. (Facilitator helps smaller children draw.)

3. After children have an outline of themselves, instruct them to draw, color, or use cut-out material pieces to do their features (eyes, mouth, hair, etc.). Instruct the children to use the hand mirror to see the placement of these features and the colors to use. Have children use pieces of material for accessories such as pockets, shoes, designs.

4. Have older children cut out their body-drawing (optional).

Facilitator: Help younger children to cut theirs. Write the name on the back of the drawing.

5. Tape or tack the body cut-outs or whole butcher paper onto the walls around the room.

Discussion: Ask children to guess which body cut-out belongs to whom. Emphasize that each child is different, even though they may have the same color of hair, eyes, or clothing as someone else. Emphasize that being different makes each child a very special person and they stay special even after they leave the group.

HEALTHY SNACK TIME
(10 minutes)

Foods: Several flavors of granola bars (oat, chocolate chip, raisin)
                Several types of juice (pineapple, orange, cranberry)

Directions: Cut granola bars into small slices. Allow children to taste all flavors. Do the same with juice. Let them judge which ones they like best individually and as a group.

Discussion: Talk about the four food groups, and where today's snack fits in the groups.

GOODBYE
(5 minutes)

Directions: Have all children sit in a circle. Allow each child to tell the group what he/she liked about the group today. Stand up and have each child shake hands goodbye with all group members.

REMEMBER THE POSITIVE DAILY MESSAGE!

ACTIVITY 2

SELF-ESTEEM

BEFORE THE SESSION	

Materials:

- Handout:
  Super Me

- Colored pencils
- Regular pencils

HELLO
What I Like About Me
(*5 minutes*)

Facilitator: Introduce yourself and the *S.K.I.T.* program. Go over the rules for being a part of the group. (Refer to Poster or Rules sheet.)

Everyone sits in a circle at the table or on the floor. Each child says his/her name the first time around. The second time around, the child says in a sentence, "My name is _____, and the thing I like the best about **me** is _____." (Facilitator starts if the group is shy.)

Example: My name is Linda and I like the color of my hair best.

REMEMBER TO REINFORCE THE POSITIVE DAILY MESSAGE WITH EACH CHILD SOMETIME DURING THE SESSION.

"YOU ARE A SMART, FUN, CARING PERSON!"
"YES, I AM!"
"IF YOU DON'T FEEL LIKE YOU ARE, FAKE IT 'TIL YOU MAKE IT!"

S.K.I.T. LEARNING ACTIVITY
(10 minutes)

Super Me

Goal: To help children discover good and positive traits about themselves. To help children describe themselves in words and phrases.

Directions:

1. Give each child a "Super Me" handout.

2. Have children color over big spots lightly with colored pencils.

3. Children or the facilitator: Write positive traits in each spot to describe that child. The first word that goes in a spot can be the word they used in the Hello section.

4. Have children write their names at the top of the page on the front side.

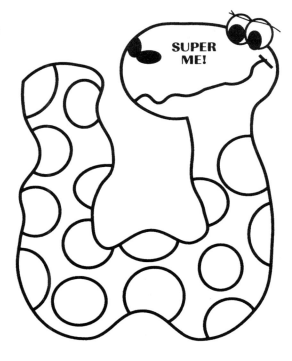

Facilitator: Pick up the activity pages and read the descriptive words aloud. Have children select the people in the group who fit each word, even if he/she is not the one who completed the sheet.

READING/ RELAXATION
(10 minutes)

Willy the Worm

Facilitator: Read the following story. Pictures of cocoons and butterflies will help children create visual images.

Willy the Worm Becomes a Butterfly

One time there was a worm, born to a mom and a dad. His name was Willy the Worm. Willy's parents felt that Willy was different because he was all different colors. He was red, brown, yellow, freckled with spots and stripes. Really, Willy was just special.

When Willy first realized he was alive and different was when he noticed that his brothers and sisters were all black, all brown, or all white. They all made fun of him because he did not look anything like the other members of his family.

When Willy the Worm grew up and went out to make a living, he was still different from the others. He ate things like tree leaves, grass, and leaves from bushes.

Willie climbed a tree, looking for happiness. He had seen a tree way, way down in the valley. He crawled to the tree way, way down in the valley. When he got there, he found a whole bunch of other worms there. Willy the Worm climbed and climbed, getting stepped on and mashed. While climbing to the top, he met another worm who looked a little bit like him because he was also different colors. His name was Sam.

READING/ RELAXATION *(cont'd)*

They became friends. Sam told Willy that he had already been to the top and there was nothing there. Willy didn't believe him, so he kept climbing. When he did get to the top, there was nothing but a lot of other worms, so he started back down. One day when he was crawling up another tree to eat the leaves from the top, he saw a beautiful colored butterfly. This butterfly recognized Willy and said, "Don't you remember me? I'm Sam, your friend." Willy said, "Sam, you look so different—you look beautiful! How did you do it?" Sam replied, "Well, it was really hard work, but I will tell you how."

So, Willy began to spin a home for himself, covering himself in a web. He completely sealed himself into the web, as Sam told him to do. (Ask children what this web is called.) Several months later, Willy worked harder and harder to push himself out of the cocoon. There he was, a beautiful butterfly. Willy the Worm, that no one liked because of his ugliness, became Willy the Beautiful Butterfly.

Tell the children: "All of us are special. We all are different from others, which makes us special."

Discussion: Have children compare eye colors and hair colors. Talk about how special we each are, even though we have some traits that are alike. When someone is different from you, do you make fun of them? Tell them again how special they are.

HEALTHY SNACK TIME
(10 minutes)

Foods: Fruit chewies (real fruit snacks)
               Lemonade

Directions: Pass out snack. Talk about the different flavors of the fruit and how they look different in color (and perhaps shape). Just as we are different, the shapes of the fruit chewies are different and each piece of fruit is special.

Discussion: Talk about the importance of eating fruits and veggies every day.

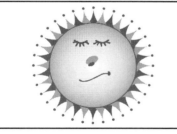

GOODBYE
(5 minutes)

Directions: Have all children sit in a circle. Allow each child to repeat the one special feature they gave in the Hello Activity. Tell them to add other special features that they discovered about themselves during the session.

REMEMBER THE POSITIVE DAILY MESSAGE!

ACTIVITY 3
DECISION-MAKING

BEFORE THE SESSION	

Materials:

- Balloons (enough for all children)
- VCR or Video Projector
- Video on decision-making skills (20–30 min. long)

HELLO
Name Train
(5 minutes)

Facilitator: Introduce yourself and the *S.K.I.T.* program. Go over the rules for being a part of the group. (Refer to Poster or Rules sheet.)

(IN ORDER TO DO THIS GAME, THERE MUST BE A MINIMUM OF FOUR CHILDREN IN THE GROUP. If there are fewer than four, use another Hello Activity.)

Directions: Have everyone stand in a circle, facing the center. Have one player volunteer (or choose someone if no one does) to be the locomotive. The locomotive acts the part of chugging around the circle with his/her arm moving up and down, choo-chooing, and maybe letting off a blast like a steam whistle. The locomotive stops in front of one of the other children in the circle and exchanges introductions.

Example: "Hi, I'm Bob R." The other child responds with, "Hi, I'm Mary."

35

HELLO   *(cont'd)*

Upon learning the child's name, the other members of the circle chant the name as if choo-chooing (Mary! Mary! Mary! Mary!).

After Mary has been hailed, Bob the locomotive turns around, Mary places her hands on his shoulders as a caboose, and the two of them chug around across the circle to select another member to ask. When another train car (child) is selected, the process is repeated, but Mary becomes the locomotive, Bob the middle train car, and the new child is the caboose.

The group continues to add train cars, cheering everyone by name. Trains may split into two trains if there are enough children.

REMEMBER TO REINFORCE THE POSITIVE DAILY MESSAGE WITH EACH CHILD SOMETIME DURING THE SESSION.

"YOU ARE A SMART, FUN, CARING PERSON!"
"YES, I AM!"
"IF YOU DON'T FEEL LIKE YOU ARE,
FAKE IT 'TIL YOU MAKE IT!"

GAME/ EXERCISE ACTIVITY
(10 minutes)

Balloon Volley

Directions: **Team Volley:** Divide into two or three teams with each team getting a balloon. The team must work together to keep the balloon from hitting the ground. Each time the team's balloon touches the ground, record a mark on the blackboard or paper. The team with the **least** marks wins. Next

36

GAME
EXERCISE *(cont'd)*
ACTIVITY

---

game, the team with the **most** marks wins. (Don't tell them the twist!) Make sure each team wins.

Individual Volley: Each child is given a balloon. The object is to see how many times the child can tap the balloon to keep it in the air before it hits the floor. (Optional: record each child's score on the blackboard for each child to better their own score.) Allow children to take balloons with them at the end of the session.

S.K.I.T. LEARNING
ACTIVITY
(20–30 minutes)

Decision-Making Skills

Goal: To guide children in learning to make decisions.

Directions: Select a video that shows decision-making skills as a focus. Film should not be more than 20–30 minutes in length. Have children sit on the floor or in chairs (no lying down). Introduce the "show." Tell children to try to recognize when someone is making a decision.

Discussion: After the "show," ask children what some of the decisions were that the people in the film had to make. Did they make the right choice? Ask what they liked best about the show. What didn't they like about the show?

Note: Serve the popcorn for Healthy Snack Time during the video, like a real movie!

HEALTHY SNACK TIME
(10 minutes)

Foods: Popcorn (prepared in an air popper)
Water

Directions: Serve during the *S.K.I.T.* Learning Activity. For a twist, spray the popcorn with cooking spray while it's still hot, sprinkle it with Parmesan cheese, and the cheese will stick!

Discussion: Talk about ways to make a "junk food" snack healthy.

Example: Making popcorn in an air popper instead of using oil.

GOODBYE
(5 minutes)

Directions: Have all children sit in a circle, Indian-style, knees touching. Explain that the time for the day is gone. Have each one tell what their favorite part of the session was today.

REMEMBER THE POSITIVE DAILY MESSAGE!

ACTIVITY 4
DECISION-MAKING

BEFORE THE SESSION

Materials:

- Different colored dots
- Drawing paper
- Pencils
- Paint brushes
- Elmer's glue in several small bottles or dishes
- Cereals (Chex, Fruit Loops, or other designs—large pieces)
- A picture of a baby elephant *(helpful)*

HELLO
Colored Dots
(5 minutes)

Facilitator: Introduce yourself and the *S.K.I.T.* program. Discuss the rules for being a part of the group. (Refer to Poster or Rules page.)

Have everyone sit in a circle. Talk about the group rules. Give each child a dot that is either red, yellow, green, or blue. (Use fewer colors if there are fewer children.) Children with the same color of dot split up, sit together, and tell each other their name and what job they would like to do when they grow up. After everyone has had a chance to share this information, have the group return to the big circle. Have one member of each of the groups volunteer to tell about the other members of the group.

REMEMBER TO REINFORCE THE POSITIVE DAILY MESSAGE WITH EACH CHILD SOMETIME DURING THE SESSION.

"YOU ARE A SMART, FUN, CARING PERSON!"
"YES, I AM!"
"IF YOU DON'T FEEL LIKE YOU ARE, FAKE IT 'TIL YOU MAKE IT!"

39

S.K.I.T. LEARNING ACTIVITY
(10 minutes)

Cereal Art

Goal:　　　To encourage creativeness and decision-making through the use of various materials.

Directions:　1. Each child receives a piece of paper and a pencil. Glue and cereal are shared by all. Instruct children to draw a large object such as a flower, boat, house, circle, square. Help smaller children.

　　　　　　2. Use paint brushes to paint the glue on the lines of the drawing.

　　　　　　3. Let children put the cereal on the glue to make a picture. They can either make an outline or fill in the whole picture. Let them make the decision.

Discussion:　Ask the children if they know what "decision-making" means. Have them discuss how it felt to be making decisions on their own.

READING/ RELAXATION
(10–15 minutes)

Elephants Can Make Your Stomach Hurt!

Facilitator: Have the children lie flat on their backs. Tell the following story.

Hey! Here comes a cute baby elephant. But he is not watching where he is going. He's about to step on your stomach! Don't move, but get ready for him.

Make your stomach really tight. It looks like he is going away. You can relax now. Let your stomach go. Let it be very soft and relaxed. That feels so much better.

Oops! He's coming back this way again. Get ready. Tighten up your stomach.... really hard, like a rock. If he steps on you when your stomach is hard, it won't hurt. Make it really hard. Okay, he turned around and left. You can relax now. Settle down, get very comfortable, and make your stomach soft like a pillow.

This time he is really coming this way. He's headed straight for you! Tighten up, tighten hard. Here he comes. You've got to hold on tight. Now he's gone for good. You can relax completely. You are safe. Everything is okay.

READING/ RELAXATION *(cont'd)*

Now imagine that you want to squeeze through a narrow fence and the boards have splinters on them. You have to make yourself very skinny. Squeeze your stomach against your back very tightly. Try to be as skinny as you can. You got through, so now you can rest. Just relax and let your stomach go back to normal size.

Let's try to get through that fence again. Get as skinny as you can. Hold tight, really tight. You made it through again! You can relax. Settle back and let your stomach come back out.

Discussion: Ask the children how their stomachs felt when they were relaxed and tight. Which felt better?

HEALTHY SNACK TIME
(10 minutes)

Foods: Peanut butter
Assorted crackers
Apple juice (100%)

Directions: Do a taste test with the crackers. Have the group pick their favorite cracker with or without peanut butter on it.

Discussion: Talk about the "hidden" fats in some foods, like peanut butter and crackers.

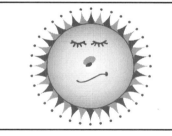

GOODBYE
(5 minutes)

Directions: Have all children sit Indian-style in a circle, knees touching. Explain that the time for today is over. Have each child tell what his/her favorite part of the session was today.

REMEMBER THE POSITIVE DAILY MESSAGE!

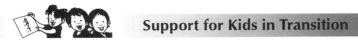

NOTES:

ACTIVITY 5

FAMILY AND FRIENDS

BEFORE THE SESSION

Materials:

• Handout:
Family Puppets

• Hokey Pokey record or tape (if you cannot get this, use another dance-type tape/record that encourages friendship and cooperation)

• Markers or crayons

• Scissors

• Glue

• Craft sticks or throat culture sticks or thick pipe cleaners

HELLO
My Family
(5 minutes)

Facilitator: Introduce yourself and the *S.K.I.T.* program. Discuss the rules for being a part of the group. (Refer to Poster or Rules page.)

Go over the group rules. Have children sit in a circle or at a round table. Have each one introduce him/herself by saying their whole name—first, middle, and last. After the full name is given, each child tells what name he/she prefers to be called. After going around the circle, each child then tells something about his/her family that they wish to share, such as number of brothers and sisters, names, etc. After going around the circle, each child will then tell what he/she likes about the family and does not like about the family.

REMEMBER TO REINFORCE THE POSITIVE DAILY MESSAGE WITH EACH CHILD SOMETIME DURING THE SESSION.

"YOU ARE A SMART, FUN, CARING PERSON!"
"YES, I AM!"
"IF YOU DON'T FEEL LIKE YOU ARE, FAKE IT 'TIL YOU MAKE IT!"

45

GAME/
EXERCISE ACTIVITY
(5–10 minutes)

The Hokey Pokey Dance

Directions: Act out the Hokey Pokey Dance. Play over again up to five times.

Words: You put your left hand in, you put your left hand out. You put your left hand in, and you shake it all about. You do the Hokey Pokey and you turn yourself around, that's what it's all about!

(repeat with right hand, left arm, right arm, left foot, right foot, left leg, right leg, whole self)

S.K.I.T. LEARNING ACTIVITY

(30–35 minutes)

Family Puppets

Goal: There are many different kinds of family units. As children become more aware of this, they can be more understanding and accepting of differences.

Directions:

1. The facilitator explains that there are many different kinds of families: divorced, separated, kids in foster care, adopted family, blended, death in the family, substance abuse, etc. Discuss any type that children do not understand. Explain that families are places where a group of people live or a group of people that are close (families are not always made up of blood relatives). There is no one family better than another. They are all different.

2. Give each child the family handout pages according to who they wish to put in their family unit.

3. Allow children to color family member heads and cut out if they are old enough. Have some pre-cut for those who cannot do this or if you do not have time.

4. Have the children place glue at the top portion of the stick and lay the colored cut-out head in place.

5. While glue is drying, have children sing a song about families (select a song from a tape or record they all know).

Example: *We Are Fam-i-ly*

Discussion: Stress again that each family is different. Have each child, who offers, take his family puppet and act out a scene which describes the family. Facilitator may start with his/her own puppets to get things started.

HEALTHY SNACK TIME
(10 minutes)

Foods: Nuts (pecans, almonds, walnuts, cashews) in separate bowls
Tang orange drink

Directions: Have children taste each kind of nut and determine which ones they like best.

Discussion: Show a chart or drawing which shows the nut, its name, and something interesting about it.

Example: Why are peanuts called <u>pea</u>-<u>nuts</u>?

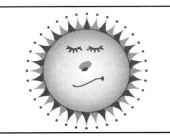

GOODBYE
(5 minutes)

Directions: Have all children sit in a circle and tell the group something really special about a friend or family member. They can use their puppets to explain their feelings during this goodbye.

REMEMBER THE POSITIVE DAILY MESSAGE!

FAMILY PUPPETS

Mother

Brother

Father

49

FAMILY PUPPETS

Grandmother

Sister

Baby

Grandfather

ACTIVITY 6
FAMILY AND FRIENDS

BEFORE THE SESSION	

Materials:

- Handout: *Picture of My Family*
- Markers
- Scissors
- Glue
- Construction paper— large size if possible
- Magazines
- Birthday candles (optional)
- Marshmallows
- Straws with paper flames

HELLO
Names, Names, Names
(5 minutes)

Facilitator: Introduce yourself and the *S.K.I.T.* program. Discuss the rules for being a part of the group. (Refer to Poster or Rules page.)

Have all children sit in a circle. Each child says his first name three times and his last name three times. After all children have repeated their names, go around the circle again, but this time the first child must give the name of the child to the right of him/her.

When all names have been repeated, ask the group if it was easier to remember the names by repeating the name three times, or if it was harder. Facilitator must now go around the circle and repeat each child's first **or** last name.

REMEMBER TO REINFORCE THE POSITIVE DAILY MESSAGE WITH EACH CHILD SOMETIME DURING THE SESSION.

"YOU ARE A SMART, FUN, CARING PERSON!"
"YES, I AM!"
"IF YOU DON'T FEEL LIKE YOU ARE, FAKE IT 'TIL YOU MAKE IT!"

51

S.K.I.T. LEARNING ACTIVITY
(30–35 minutes)

Family and Friends Are Special

Goal: All families have characteristics that make them special. This exercise will help children recognize the specialness of their own family.

Directions:
1. Discuss with the children different activities that families do together. Suggestions: watch TV, sports, walks, talks, reading, etc.

2. On the Picture of My Family handout, have children draw a picture in the circle with a marker of their family doing something that they like to do, have done in the past month, or would like to see their family do.

3. Have children cut out family circle and glue to the center of the construction paper.

4. Have children, or help the smaller ones, cut out small magazine pictures of families or members of a family doing things together and glue on the construction paper **around** the circle.

Discussion: Stress to children how families do special activities together in different ways.

READING/ RELAXATION
(15 minutes)

A Gift of Feelings

Directions: Read the following story aloud. A sample of a page or a whole book written in braille will enhance the story. If you are really creative, construct a book similar to the one in the story. Pass this around while reading the story.

A GIFT OF FEELINGS by Barbara Schenck

Matt slowly counted the money in his hand. Two dollars and seven cents. No matter how many times he counted it, it was the same. And it was never enough. He stuffed the coins back in his pocket and sat leaning against the oak tree, staring at the sky. The book catalog under his arm dropped to the ground. He had wanted to buy his brother Steve a book for his birthday—a braille book because Steve was blind and was just learning to read braille.

"He's never had a book he could read himself," Matt told his mother. "His own—to keep, I mean." His mother nodded. "I know," she said. "You read so much to him, though, Matt. He likes that. And braille books are expensive. He's only going to be eight. There will be time for his own books later on." She laid a hand on Matt's shoulder and smiled at him.

Matt knew she was right. Steve did like it when Matt read him books and stories. But Matt also remembered something his mother did not. One night after he had finished reading to Steve, his brother remained still for a very long time. Then he said, "You really love that story, don't you, Matt?"

READING\ RELAXATION   *(cont'd)*

Matt looked at the worn, often-turned pages. "Yes," he said.

"And it's there any time you want to read it." Steve's voice was getting excited and he sat up. "Yes," Matt agreed.

"I wish I had a book," Steve said simply, and then he lay back down. "I wish I had a book that I could pick up and make the story come alive again, too. All these books are the same for me."

So it had to be a book—a braille book—because regular ones all felt alike to someone who could not see to read the words.

Suddenly, Matt sat upright. That's it, he thought!! If a book didn't feel like the rest—even if it weren't a real braille book—wouldn't Steve be really able to know that book? His excitement grew, and the more he thought about the idea, the more he knew what he would do.

For the next few weeks, Matt disappeared after school. He had a lot of work to do before Steve's birthday. During that exciting month, he visited Steve's braille teacher, Mr. Gage, the librarian at the public library, and the hardware and art supply stores, and soon he had everything he needed to begin work.

READING\ RELAXATION *(cont'd)*

Finally, the day of Steve's birthday arrived. That Sunday morning, Matt was awake even before his brother. He got up quietly, dressed, and slipped outside to his dad's workshop. There he checked over Steve's present once again. Then he carefully wrapped the package. Tucking it under his arm, he went back into the house.

His mother was making waffles, Steve's favorite. "Good morning," she said with a smile. "Is that for Steve?" Matt nodded. He put it on the table by his brother's place with the other gifts. "Where's Steve?" Matt asked. "Right here!" Dad answered as he opened the door to the kitchen. He and Steve came in smiling.

"Happy Birthday!" Matt said. He caught his brother by the arm. "Do you want your eight swats now or later?" Steve laughed. "Just try to get them!" Then, sniffing, he said, "Mmm, waffles!" "Aren't you going to open your presents?" Dad said.

Steve went to his chair. He began opening his gifts as Matt handed them to him, reserving his own for last. Mom and Dad gave Steve a jacket, and a sack of red clay because he loved to make things with his hands. From his grandfather came the knapsack Steve had talked about but never dreamed of getting. At last Matt handed him a flat box. "This one's from me," he said. "Be careful. Don't just rip into it!"

READING\ RELAXATION   *(cont'd)*

"OK," Steve said. Slowly and deliberately, he removed the wrapping. Mom and Dad looked at Matt questioningly. He smiled slightly at them but turned to watch his brother. Steve took the lid off the box and lifted out his gift. His hands moved slowly over it.

" A book," he breathed. His hands brushed the posterboard cover. "Hey!" he exclaimed. "Letters! I can feel letters. Is it sandpaper or what?" He stopped and slowly traced the letters on the cover—sandpaper letters spelling STEVE. And after he had done it once, he did it again.

"It's **my** book," he said joyously, opening the first page. On heavy paper there were raised cut-out cardboard outlines of four people: a man, a woman, and two boys. Steve's story, as Matt had written it carefully in newly learned braille, began at the bottom of the page.

Stumbling a bit, Steve read the two or three sentences on each page. He read that he always had eaten more graham crackers than Matt when he was little, and he felt the graham cracker Matt had glued on that page. One page recalled their vacation at the beach and had sand, pebbles, and shells on it. Another told briefly of Uncle Bill's farm with glued-on corn, soybeans, and straw. On each page Matt had told the story in braille and, as Dad said, "with illustrations."

"I've got a book," Steve said as he closed the last page. "And it really is my own story. I can read it again and again, and I can keep it forever." He turned to where Matt was sitting at the table watching him. "Oh, Matt,

READING\ RELAXATION *(cont'd)*

thank you. It's the best gift ever!" Matt looked at Steve's smiling face, at his hands which still moved quietly over the cover, and knew it had been worth it. Steve's own book was worth every hour Matt had spent learning the braille alphabet, every error he had made transcribing the story with the stylus Mr. Gage had shown him how to use, every new beginning to make Steve's story simple, yet alive and able to be felt and read by his brother alone.

"It was fun, Steve," Matt said. "I'm glad that I made it. Maybe together we can make you a whole library!"

Discussion: Ask the children: What made the book so special? Have them think of special things they can do for people they love.

HEALTHY SNACK TIME
(10 minutes)

Foods: Apple slices
                Yogurt (3 flavors)
                Water with a slice of lemon (optional)

Directions: Cut apples into small sections. Have the children dip apples into the
                different yogurt flavors. Take a poll on which they like best.

Discussion: Talk about the importance of drinking lots of water every day.

GOODBYE
(5 minutes)

Directions: Have children sit in a circle on the floor, Indian-style. Give each child a
                large marshmallow with a candle stuck in it. As each child says something
                special about his/her family, the facilitator lights the candle. All blow out
                the candles at the same time. (Be sure to collect candles for another time.)

Note: Do not use candles if children are too hyperactive or too young. Instead,
                stick a straw with a paper flame on the top in the marshmallow and have
                them pretend it is a candle.

REMEMBER THE POSITIVE DAILY MESSAGE!

PICTURE OF MY FAMILY

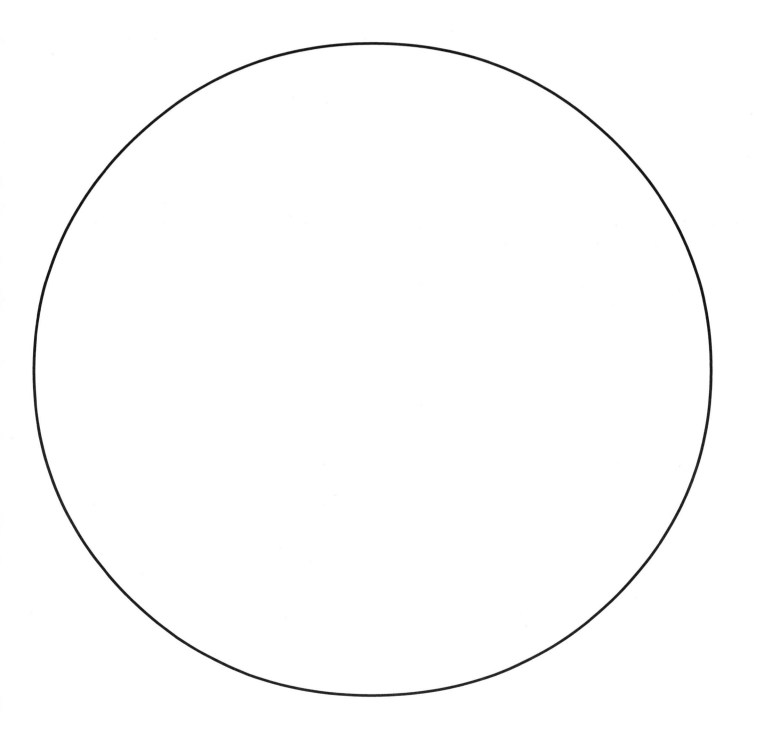

NOTES:

ACTIVITY 7
CHEMICAL DEPENDENCY

BEFORE THE SESSION

Materials:

- Handouts:
  Flower
  Substance Abuse Messages

- Markers
- Scissors
- Glue
- Construction paper
- Pipe cleaner bees (found in craft store)
- Magnet and piece of metal (for illustration only)
- Masking tape

HELLO
Names in Motion
(5 minutes)

Facilitator: Introduce yourself and the *S.K.I.T.* program. Discuss the rules for being a part of the group. (Refer to Poster or Rules page.)

Each child will share his/her name and a special motion with the group.

Example: Saying name and waving hello, or saying name while snapping fingers.

The group repeats the first child's name and motion. Continue until each child has stated their name and motion, and the whole group has repeated it.

REMEMBER TO REINFORCE THE POSITIVE DAILY MESSAGE WITH EACH CHILD SOMETIME DURING THE SESSION.

"YOU ARE A SMART, FUN, CARING PERSON!"
"YES, I AM!"
"IF YOU DON'T FEEL LIKE YOU ARE, FAKE IT 'TIL YOU MAKE IT!"

GAME/ EXERCISE ACTIVITY
(5–10 minutes)

People to People

Directions: Each child chooses a partner. Designate a caller, who will call out two body parts at a time (*Example:* Toe to Knee). One of the pair must try to touch his first body part with the second body part of the other child.

Example: Elbow to knee; head to back; finger to foot; feet to feet; etc.

After three or four different calls, the caller says, "People to People." Everyone must change partners. The caller becomes one of the players. The odd person out now becomes the caller and he/she calls out two body parts. Repeat three to four times and call, "People to People." Change partners.

Note: There is no solution to re-enact these combinations. It's fun to see how each pair interprets them differently.

BE CREATIVE—KIDS LOVE THIS GAME!

S.K.I.T. LEARNING ACTIVITY
(30–35 minutes)

Flower Pot

Goal: To explain alcohol/drug addiction and chemical dependency to young children in a non-judgmental manner.

Directions:

1. On a large piece of paper or blackboard, write the word "Addicted." Let children tell you their conceptual meanings or ideas of what addicted means. Write their ideas in big letters around the word.

2. Give each child the handout of the flower pattern and scissors for cutting out patterns. Help smaller children cut or pre-cut these before the session.

3. Have children draw the pattern on felt and cut out felt flower pieces. Children may cut flower out of many colors or one color, and stem may be cut as well. *Option:* If group is primarily composed of small children, or to save time, you may want to have pieces already cut out.

4. Have children glue flower pieces to the flower, and the flower to a piece of construction paper.

5. Explain to the children through visual illustration that
   • Paper sticks to glue.
   • Magnets stick to metal.
   • Bees stick to flowers.

S.K.I.T.
LEARNING *(cont'd)*
ACTIVITY

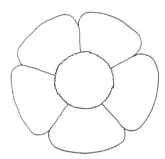

6. Explain that an alcoholic or drug addict is stuck to alcohol or drugs. There is a word for this: **Addicted.** It is a habit that is very hard to break, and often becomes a **need** for a person, just like eating food.

Glue the **bee** to the center of each child's flower. Have them wait a few minutes, until the **bees** are stuck, and then ask them to try to pull the **bee** off.

Discussion: Explain that when someone we know is a substance abuser, we sometimes get confused about how they feel about us and how we feel about them. Sometimes people who drink too much, or use drugs, change from being nice to being mean, or from giving a lot of attention to wanting to be alone. Sometimes what people do when they are drinking or on drugs is the opposite of how they really feel. The substance (alcohol, drugs) makes them act differently.

If someone in the family is addicted, we aren't sure if we love them at all sometimes. We may even hate them during those times. We may think that they hate us. At a certain moment we might really hate them or be mad at them, but deep inside we might still love them. Have the children share other beliefs and feelings with the group.

HEALTHY SNACK TIME
(10 minutes)

Foods: String cheese or other types of cheese
100% juice and 10% juice drinks

Directions: Have children do a taste test to see which juice they like better. Give each child a small cup of 100% and 10% juice. Take a vote. (You will probably find that more than 50% like real juice drinks.)

Discussion: Talk about the importance of moderation in eating some good foods.

Example: Cheese has protein (good), but it also has fat (bad).

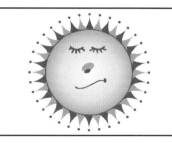

GOODBYE
(5 minutes)

Directions: Using masking tape, tape all children together in a circle. Explain how chemical dependency/addiction affects all members of a family or group.

When one person moves, everyone shifts or the tape breaks. This is often painful. Have children move around trying not to break the tape. Then have them move rapidly and see what happens. When someone in the family is addicted, it often breaks the family up. Have everyone share what they liked and did not like about the session.

REMEMBER THE POSITIVE DAILY MESSAGE!

FLOWER

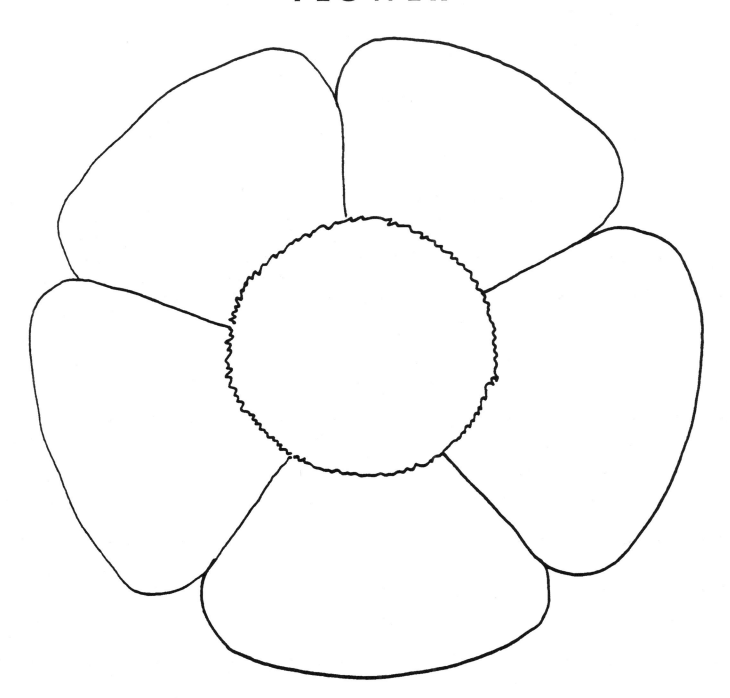

SUBSTANCE ABUSE MESSAGES

1. YOU ARE NOT ALONE.

2. THE DRINKING OR DRUG USE OF A FAMILY MEMBER IS NOT YOUR FAULT.

3. SUBSTANCE ADDICTION IS AN ILLNESS.

4. SUBSTANCE ADDICTS CAN RECOVER, BUT IT IS THEIR CHOICE.

5. YOU CAN GET HELP FOR YOURSELF.

NOTES:

ACTIVITY 8

CHEMICAL DEPENDENCY

BEFORE THE SESSION	

Materials:

- Wallpaper, construction paper, sandpaper, paper plates, etc.
- All types of natural materials such as seeds, feathers, leaves, pretty rocks, seashells
- Textured items such as sandpaper, satin, cotton, string, etc.
- Smelly items such as cinnamon sticks, cloves, soap bits, etc.
- Glue, tape, and scissors

HELLO
Barn Animals
(5 minutes)

Facilitator: Introduce yourself and the *S.K.I.T.* program. Discuss the rules for being a part of the group. (Refer to Poster or Rules page.)

Have children sit in a circle on the floor. One child begins by making a sound like a barn animal. The others guess what the animal is. The child who made the sound must then attach his/her first name to that animal.

Example: John Cow, Maria Chicken.

This continues around the circle until all animals have names. The facilitator tries to go around the room naming all first names and animal last names. Children who want to try may do the same.

REMEMBER TO REINFORCE THE POSITIVE DAILY MESSAGE WITH EACH CHILD SOMETIME DURING THE SESSION.

"YOU ARE A SMART, FUN, CARING PERSON!"
"YES, I AM!"
"IF YOU DON'T FEEL LIKE YOU ARE, FAKE IT 'TIL YOU MAKE IT!"

S.K.I.T. LEARNING ACTIVITY
(30 minutes)

Sensory Collages

Goal: To give children a wide range of sensory experiences.

Directions:
1. Have children create collages on their own that combine texture, smell, and natural materials.

2. Explain to the children that it is not necessary to make a picture, just a collage that expresses a good feeling.

3. After the collages are complete, have the children tell why they feel good when they look at, smell, and feel their collage. Ask children what things they have that make them feel good.

Example: An old teddy bear, hugs, pat on the back.

4. Have the children talk about the kind of collage they could make that would make them feel bad.

Example: I would first take black paper, sprinkle some pepper on it that would make me sneeze, then I would spray some insect spray on the paper that would smell really bad.

Discussion: Have the children discuss what they do to feel happy at times they feel really sad or mad.

Example: When I feel mad, I go to my room and feel my baseball glove and that makes me feel good.

READING/ RELAXATION
(10 minutes)

The Rabbit Who Couldn't Stop Eating

Directions: Have the children sit in a circle. Before telling this story, the facilitator should first discuss the word "Addiction" and substance abuse, which is found in Activity 7. Have children give examples of addictions and substances that are often abused. Explain to children that they will be filling the story as you tell it.

Name one child who will be responsible for filling in the first blank, and then go clockwise around the circle for answers to the remaining blanks. If a child does not want to fill in the blank, move on to the next child.

Note: If there is a tape recorder, it is fun to tape the story and play it back at the end so the children can hear the whole story.

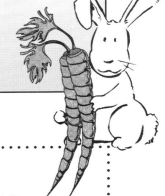

READING/ RELAXATION *(cont'd)*

THE RABBIT WHO COULDN'T STOP EATING

Joey was a little white rabbit who lived in the woods near a very big farm. Every day Joey would hop over to the farm because there was a very big garden.

He would hop over the fence and the first thing he would do is eat the _____ that were in the garden. He ate and ate the _____. In fact, some days he ate so many that he became _____. The other rabbits tried to tell him that he was eating too many _____.

Joey's mama, who was a big gray rabbit, told him that she was afraid that if he kept eating so many _____ that he would turn into a _____. Joey didn't want to listen to the other _____. He began to stay by himself and _____. He was so lonely that he started to stay at the garden all the time and he even ate more _____. It seemed like all those _____ he ate became his only friends.

One day Joey decided that if he really wanted to be happy, he would need to stop eating so many _____. He tried not to go to the garden but it was very hard. He really wanted some more _____.

Joey then asked the other rabbits to help him not go to the garden. Every place the rabbits went, Joey went along. Pretty soon, he forgot

READING/ RELAXATION *(cont'd)*

all about the garden and the _____. He started
eating like all the other _____ and started to have
more fun and friends.

Discussion: Ask the children the following questions:

1. What was Joey addicted to?

2. Did it make him happy to eat so many _____?

3. What helped him to get over his addiction to _____?

4. Review the other kinds of addictions that there are with the children.
Let children take the conversation from this point.

HEALTHY SNACK TIME
(10 minutes)

Foods: Sliced carrots, celery, cucumbers
Ranch-style dip
Juice

Directions: Cut vegetables into pieces that can easily be dipped. Have children tell which vegetables they like the best. If there are children that do not want to try, have the children who do tell what tastes so good about that vegetable.

Discussion: This snack fits very well with the story about rabbits. Talk with the children about this theme.

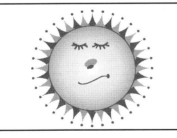

GOODBYE
(5 minutes)

Directions: Have the children sit in a circle and tell what part of the session they liked the best. Have them hold hands and give a good squeeze.

REMEMBER THE POSITIVE DAILY MESSAGE!

AGES 6 THRU 9

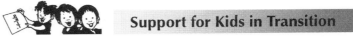

Support for Kids in Transition

ACTIVITY 1
SELF-ESTEEM

BEFORE THE SESSION	

Materials:

- Plastic name tag covers
- Index cards or stiff paper cut to fit the tags
- Markers or colored pencils
- Glue and glitter
- 1 decorated shoe box with a mirror glued inside (prepare in advance)
- Additional shoe boxes, enough for each child
- Markers, glitter, glue, buttons, flashy trim, magazine pictures, wrapping paper, etc.

Preparation Needed in Advance:

Decorate a shoe box according to the diagram on page 81.

HELLO
Who I Want To Be
(5 minutes)

Facilitator: Introduce yourself and the *S.K.I.T.* program. Rules for being part of the group are discussed. (Rules should already be made into signs or posters and hung on the wall.) If the group wants to add rules for the sessions they can as long as the entire group agrees, including you.

Directions: Have children sit in a circle on the floor or at a table. Each child is to say his name and the names of one man and one woman who are famous that he/she likes. Explain that they can be an actor, a president, a cartoon character, or some other person. Have each child tell why they would like to be those two persons in one sentence.

HELLO *(cont'd)*

*REMEMBER TO REINFORCE THE POSITIVE DAILY MESSAGE
WITH EACH CHILD SOMETIME DURING THE SESSION.*

*"YOU ARE A SMART, FUN,
CARING PERSON!"*
"YES, I AM!"
*"IF YOU DON'T FEEL LIKE YOU ARE,
FAKE IT 'TIL YOU MAKE IT!"*

GAME/ EXERCISE ACTIVITY
(5–10 minutes)

Famous Person Name Tags

Directions: On already-cut index cards, have children print the name of one of the favorite persons who they selected previously. Tell them that for the rest of the day they will be that famous person. Have them decorate the tag.

S.K.I.T. LEARNING ACTIVITY
(30–35 minutes)

The Special Box

Goal: To help children recognize their facial characteristics and feel good about themselves.

Directions: 1. Have children sit in a circle. Show all of the children the "Special Box." Before each child looks in the box, explain that there is a picture of a very important person inside the box. Explain further that this person is funny, caring, and smart.

2. Tell the children that they will each get a turn to look inside the box, but they **must not** tell anyone else what they saw.

Discussion: After showing the box to each child, discuss with the children their thoughts and feelings about this experience by asking the following questions:
- What did you see when you looked inside the box?
- How did you feel when you looked inside the box? (Tell them to pick from these words: sad, mad, glad, happy, scared.)
- What did you think of when you looked inside the box?
- Were you surprised at who you saw?
- Did you all see something different?
- How can each one of you be the most special?
- How does it make you feel to know that you are special?

Give each child his/her own box to decorate, which they will call the "**Me Box.**" Tell them to put their name somewhere on the box and then color and decorate the box in the most beautiful way they can imagine.

Tell them that they can store all of their important keepsakes in this box when they get home.

HEALTHY SNACK TIME
(5–10 minutes)

Foods: Bagel chips or mini-bagels
Cream cheese pre-mixed with strawberries, pineapple
Water or milk

Directions: Take a poll about which flavor of cream cheese the children like best.
Discuss the results.

Discussion: Talk about the importance of drinking lots of water every day.

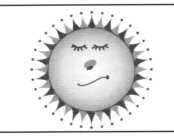

GOODBYE
(5 minutes)

Discussion: Have children sit in a circle with their "**star**" name tags and "**me**" boxes. Each child should tell how he/she is like the famous person that they selected at the beginning of the session. Have each child tell one quality about themselves that really makes them special. As a facilitator, make sure that you reinforce that quality by agreeing and complimenting the child.

REMEMBER THE POSITIVE DAILY MESSAGE!

THE SPECIAL BOX — DIAGRAM

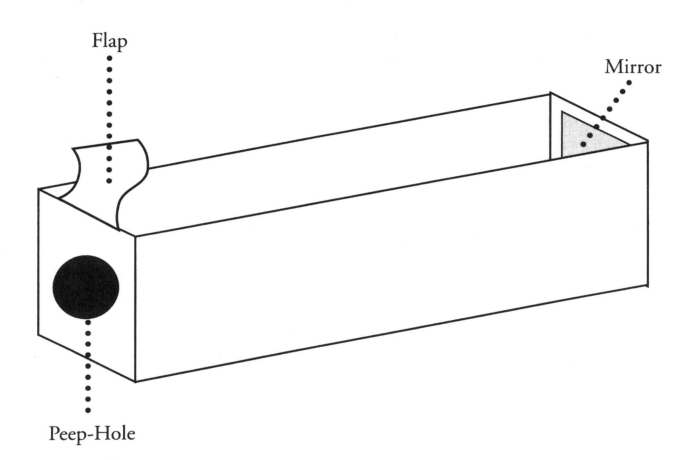

Flap

Mirror

Peep-Hole

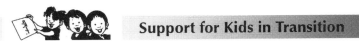
NOTES:

ACTIVITY 2
SELF-ESTEEM

BEFORE THE SESSION	

Materials:

• Handout:
A Story About Me

• Marking pens/crayons
• Scissors
• Stapler

HELLO
Animal Sounds
(5 minutes)

Facilitator: Introduce yourself and the *S.K.I.T.* program. Discuss the rules for being a part of the group. (Refer to Poster or Rules page.)

Directions: Everyone stands in a circle. Whisper in each child's ear the name of an animal (use chicken, dog, and pig). Tell the children that they must not tell others which animal they are to be. After each child has been given the name of one of the three animals, the facilitator asks the group to all make the sound of the animal that they were given at the same time. Have them repeat the sound over and over.

As the children walk around making their animal's noise, tell them to group together, pigs in one corner, dogs in one corner, and chickens in one corner. After they have grouped together, have each group talk with each other about the benefits of being that animal.

HELLO *(cont'd)*

Example: A pig can play in the mud all day, a dog can do tricks, etc.

After they have discussed the benefits of being that animal, have them come back to a large circle and have each child tell why he didn't want to be that animal.

REMEMBER TO REINFORCE THE POSITIVE DAILY MESSAGE WITH EACH CHILD SOMETIME DURING THE SESSION.

"YOU ARE A SMART, FUN, CARING PERSON!"
"YES, I AM!"
"IF YOU DON'T FEEL LIKE YOU ARE,
FAKE IT 'TIL YOU MAKE IT!"

S.K.I.T. LEARNING ACTIVITY
(20–25 minutes)

A Story About Me

Goal: To help children be more aware of themselves and their positive characteristics.

Directions: 1. Each child gets a set of the three pages.

S.K.I.T. LEARNING ACTIVITY *(cont'd)*

2. Children write/draw their own story according to each page. Facilitator will have to help younger children to read. While the children are creating their books, start a discussion about the content.

3. Children cut the pages apart (or you can cut them before the session) and assemble according to the number of pages in the upper-left-hand corner.

4. Children staple the book together (or help them staple).

Discussion: Pass the books around to group members for them to read about each other. Children can take books home.

READING/ RELAXATION
(10 minutes)

The Turtle

Facilitator: Have the children sit in a circle on their hands and knees and tell them the following story. They can act out the story.

The Turtle

Pretend you are a turtle. You are sitting out on a rock by a nice, peaceful pond just relaxing in the sun. It feels nice and warm here.

Uh-oh! You sense danger! Pull your head into your shell. Try to pull your shoulders up to your ears and push your head down into your shoulders. Mold in tight. It isn't easy to be a turtle!

The danger has passed now. You can come out into the sunshine and, once again, you can relax and feel the warm feeling.

Watch out now! More danger! Hurry, pull your head back into your shell really fast. You have to be closed in tight to protect yourself.

Okay, you can relax. Stretch your neck all the way around. Doesn't that feel good? Especially after you have been all crunched-up. Now roll over on your back; you have nothing else to be afraid of because there is no more danger.

Lay on your back, like a turtle would, if he could. You are comfortable and relaxed. Now turn back into a human.

Discussion: Ask children to think of situations when they can use this exercise as a way to relax.

HEALTHY SNACK TIME
(10 minutes)

Foods: String cheese or different kinds of cheese (sharp cheddar, Monterey Jack, Swiss)
Cranberry juice

Directions: Have children try different types of cheese, or just enjoy one piece of string cheese. Take a poll to see which kind they like best.

Discussion: Talk about the importance of moderation in eating some good foods.
Example: Cheese has protein (good), but it also has fat (bad).

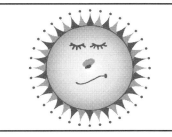

GOODBYE
(5 minutes)

Directions: Have all the children sit in a circle on the floor and tell the group what one feature of themselves they really like.

Example: I like that I can be funny.

REMEMBER THE POSITIVE DAILY MESSAGE!

A STORY ABOUT ME

Name: _____

page 2

This is what I look like.

page 3

My favorite toy is

_____.

page 4

My favorite animal is

_____.

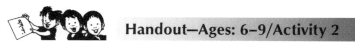

page 5

page 6

My teacher is

_____.

My favorite color is

_____.

page 7

page 8

My favorite book is

_____.

Something I don't like is

_____.

page 9

page 10

A person I love is

_____.

Here is a picture of my house.

page 11

page 12

Here is a picture of my favorite food.

Here is what I look like before I go to sleep.

THE END

GAME/ EXERCISE ACTIVITY
(5–10 minutes)

Machines

Directions: This game begins with one "machine part" and grows until all of the parts (people) have attached together to make the machine. People join in, one at a time. The facilitator may have to demonstrate first, but make sure that children do not use the same sound and motion as the facilitator.

1. Children sit/stand around the edge of the room. One person goes to the middle of the room and stands, sits, lies down, etc., and makes a single continuous motion and sound (i.e., waving arm around while making a clicking noise). Motions should be smooth and rhythmical.

2. Second person attaches to the first "machine part" in some way and makes a different sound and motion. Third person joins the machine by attaching to them, and so on, until all persons are the machine.

3. Speed up the machine (sound and movement). Have machine move around room.

   Variation: This game can be played in pairs, threes, and fours.

S.K.I.T. LEARNING ACTIVITY
(30–35 minutes)

Helping the Hurts

Goal: To help children develop the ability to determine how they deal with stress, the different methods that some people use to deal with stress, and alternative methods that children can use.

Directions:

1. Tell children that when our heads are worried or upset about something, our whole body knows it. Stress affects the whole body.

2. Have children clench their fists as tightly as they can. Have them hold this position for several seconds.

3. Ask them how it felt. How did their hands feel? (Tired, sore, tingly.) How did the rest of their body feel?

4. Pass out the "Boy" and "Girl" handouts accordingly. Explain to the children that when we hold feelings like worrying or fear or anger inside for a long time, it can hurt. Ask what happens when they are scared or nervous (i.e., stomachache, headache, tears, etc.).

5. Have children draw/mark where the aches can be found and label body aches and pains related to stress. The facilitator can demonstrate on a large boy or girl handout. These may include headaches, eye strain, stomachaches, sore throats, backache, tiredness, arm aches, etc.

6. Visually demonstrate the weight of worrying by picking up books and other objects, and explaining that these are worries about school, sickness, family problems, etc. Begin to groan and stoop under the strain of the heavy books to demonstrate stress.

S.K.I.T.
LEARNING   *(cont'd)*
ACTIVITY

---

7. Put the objects away. Explain that there are many things we can do to help our bodies and minds relax and cope better. Here are a few:

   • Have children stand in place and do the jiggle, letting arms and head flop.
   • Have children do the "guilt giggle" (giggle with no noise) when they need to feel better but not be loud.
   • Have children give examples of a time this happened when they wanted to laugh out loud but had to giggle very softly.
   • Have children laugh loud and full for when they need the pleasure of a real chuckle.
   • Have children tell something funny.
   • Have children smile at the person beside them.

8. For relaxation, have the children sit at seats or on the floor with eyes closed. Tell them to breathe deeply and slowly. Talk to them in a low, comforting voice. Tell them to relax certain parts of their bodies (heads, necks, arms, legs, feet). Have them open their eyes.

Facilitator: Tell the group that we all have worries and fears and troubles. Learning how our bodies are affected helps us understand that we need to relax. Laughter, breathing slowly and deeply, and relaxing parts of our body can help us to understand our feelings better and to control tension.

Discussion: Discuss time, events, and circumstances when children may have had worries, fears, or troubles. Discuss how the worries, fears, or troubles affected their bodies physically. Discuss how they helped deal with those times. Children can use their pictures to describe their feelings.

94

HEALTHY SNACK TIME
(10 minutes)

Foods: Yogurt—chocolate, vanilla
Shortbread cookies
Fruit juice (100%)

Directions: Have chocolate and vanilla yogurt ready for children to dip onto plain shortbread cookies.

Discussion: Talk about the everyday foods that are good sources of vitamins and minerals.

Example: Milk has vitamin D and calcium. Raisins have lots of iron.
Ask the kids if they can name any other good sources.

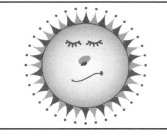

GOODBYE
(5 minutes)

Discussion: Have all the children sit in a circle. Ask them the following questions and allow all children, who wish to, time to respond:

- Would you rather play a sport or watch TV?
- Which one of those makes you feel stressful? relaxed?
- Would you rather dance and sing, or read a book?
- Do either of these make you feel stressful? relaxed?
- Did the group make you feel stressful today?
- If no, why? If yes, why?

Discuss that sometimes an activity will make one person stressful and will make another person feel relaxed.

REMEMBER THE POSITIVE DAILY MESSAGE!

95

HELPING THE HURTS

96

HELPING THE HURTS

NOTES:

ACTIVITY 3
DECISION MAKING

BEFORE THE SESSION

Materials:

- Handout: *Boy/Girl pictures*
- Crayons
- Pencils
- Star and/or dot labels

HELLO
Animal Names
(5 minutes)

Facilitator: Introduce yourself and the *S.K.I.T.* program. Discuss the rules for being a part of the group. (Refer to Poster or Rules page.)

Each child is to sit in a circle. Going around the room, each child introduces himself, each child saying only his first name the first time around. The second time around, the child says his first name and an animal name that begins with the same letter as his name (i.e., Larry-Lion). The third time around, the child must say the name of a color (i.e., Larry-Lavender). The last time, say a food. Go around one more time and have children say all of their newly created names (i.e., Larry-Lion-Lavender-Lemon).

REMEMBER TO REINFORCE THE POSITIVE DAILY MESSAGE WITH EACH CHILD SOMETIME DURING THE SESSION.

"YOU ARE A SMART, FUN, CARING PERSON!"
"YES, I AM!"
"IF YOU DON'T FEEL LIKE YOU ARE, FAKE IT 'TIL YOU MAKE IT!"

ACTIVITY 4
DECISION MAKING

BEFORE THE SESSION

Materials:

- Sheet of clues for Scavenger Hunt activity
- Paper bags for carrying hunt objects

HELLO
What I Like
(5 minutes)

Facilitator: Introduce yourself and the *S.K.I.T.* program. Discuss the rules for being a part of the group. (Refer to Poster or Rules page.)

Have the children sit in a circle. Have each child look around the room and pick something that he/she really likes. Go around the room and have children tell what they picked and why they like it.

Have children look around the room and pick something that they do not like. Have them tell why they do not like that object. Finally, go around the room and have each child give his/her first name.

REMEMBER TO REINFORCE THE POSITIVE DAILY MESSAGE WITH EACH CHILD SOMETIME DURING THE SESSION.

"YOU ARE A SMART, FUN, CARING PERSON!"
"YES, I AM!"
"IF YOU DON'T FEEL LIKE YOU ARE, FAKE IT 'TIL YOU MAKE IT!"

S.K.I.T. LEARNING ACTIVITY
(30–35 minutes)

Scavenger Hunt

Goal: To help children learn to work together as a team and make decisions collectively and individually.

Directions: 1. Clues are developed according to the ability levels of the children playing and are kept simple to allow for different choices. Children can search for clues individually or in any size group. Decide on boundaries (i.e., indoors only, outdoors only, within a yard, etc.). Write up the clue cards in advance for each group. Picture symbols can be used for non-readers. Give each person/group a bag.

2. Have children return to the group after the hunt. Allow children to line up treasures according to scavenger hunt clue list. Let them compare their "treasures." How many different objects were found from one clue? **Avoid** focusing on winners. Talk only about the objects and what the children learned during the search. Stress that one team/person having more objects than another is not important, it is what they experienced that is the focus.

Discussion: Have children talk about their "treasures" and their hunt for the treasures. Have all children return the treasures to the bags and have teams/individuals place them in a special part of the room. Do not allow children to take treasures home. Discourage any possession of them by an individual. Emphasize that these treasures have now become a part of the **group** and will remain in the group area for them to look at later. (The facilitator may choose to have the children bury the treasures in the yard for safekeeping if the items are not important. Children love to bury things!)

READING/ RELAXATION
(10 minutes)

Part A:
I Don't Know Shrug
(for tension in shoulder area)

Directions: Sitting or standing, have the children bring their shoulders to their ears and drop them quickly. While shrugging, repeat quickly and loudly, "I don't know, I don't know, I don't know." Repeat for 30 seconds.

Confidence Swing
(for tension in shoulders and positive self-talk)

Directions: Stand up, swing arms and whole body from side to side so that shoulders wrap around the whole body, rag doll style. Say loudly, "I am so smart," "I did a good job today," "I am pretty great," or other similar phrases.

Part B:

Directions: Have children lie on the floor, not touching anyone or anything. Have them continue relaxing and listen to "Free to Be…You and Me" by Marlo Thomas on the tape/album by the same name, "The Greatest Love" by Whitney Houston, or another song that emphasizes self-esteem.

HEALTHY SNACK TIME
(10 minutes)

Foods: Italian bread sticks/melba toast
Cream cheese
100% and 10% juice drinks

Directions: Have children try both the 100% and 10% juice and determine which they like best. Most likely, they will choose the 100% juice.

Discussion: Talk about the difference between 10% and 100% juice, in terms of taste and nutritional value.

GOODBYE
(5 minutes)

Directions: Have the children sit in a group circle, Indian-style. Each child is to tell what they liked best about the day. Have each child demonstrate what they will do in the future if they are feeling tense and stressful. They can show one of the exercises they learned or some other technique.

REMEMBER THE POSITIVE DAILY MESSAGE!

SUGGESTED CLUES FOR SCAVENGER HUNT

1. FIND something SMALL AND ROUND.

2. FIND something SOFT.

3. FIND something MADE OF GLASS. (Be Careful Not to Cut Yourself!)

4. FIND something BLUE.

5. FIND something that MOVES. (But Does Not Bite.)

6. FIND something SMOOTH.

7. FIND something ROUGH.

8. FIND something that is PRETTY.

9. FIND something that SMELLS SWEET.

10. FIND something you think would TASTE SOUR. (Do Not Eat It.)

11. FIND something SHINY and BRIGHT.

12. FIND something that MAKES NOISE.

GREATEST LOVE OF ALL

1st Verse: "I believe that children are the future. Teach them well and let them lead the way. Show them all the beauty they possess inside. Give them a sense of pride to make it easier. Let the children's laughter remind us how it used to be.

I decided long ago to never walk in anyone's shadow. If I fail, if I succeed, at least I lived as I believe. No matter what they take from me, they can't take away my dignity."

Chorus: "Because the greatest love of all is happening to me. Learning to love yourself is the greatest love of all. The greatest love of all is easy to achieve. Learning to love yourself is the greatest love of all."

sung by Whitney Houston

ACTIVITY 5

FAMILY AND FRIENDS

BEFORE THE SESSION

Materials:

- Handouts:
  Friends activity page
  Blank activity page

- Cassette/record "Glad to Have a Friend Like You" (Marlo Thomas— Free to Be) or other tape which sings or talks about friendship
- Twister game
- Pencils
- Scissors
- Tape
- Magazines

HELLO
My Friend
(5 minutes)

Facilitator: Introduce yourself and the *S.K.I.T.* program. Discuss the rules for being a part of the group. (Refer to Poster or Rules page.)

Have children sit in a circle on the floor. Allow each child to say his/her name and tell the name of one of his/her friends (the friend does not have to be present). Have child also tell why he/she likes that friend.

REMEMBER TO REINFORCE THE POSITIVE DAILY MESSAGE WITH EACH CHILD SOMETIME DURING THE SESSION.

"YOU ARE A SMART, FUN, CARING PERSON!"
"YES, I AM!"
"IF YOU DON'T FEEL LIKE YOU ARE, FAKE IT 'TIL YOU MAKE IT!"

GAME/
EXERCISE ACTIVITY
(10–15 minutes)

Twister

Directions: This inexpensive commercial game is hilarious for all ages. It is a body movement game played on a long sheet of plastic that is placed on the floor. Players often have to twist their bodies into unusual postures to fulfill the task at hand. Sooner or later, everyone falls on their bottoms. Instructions are inside the box.

S.K.I.T. LEARNING ACTIVITY
(30–35 minutes)

Family and Friends

Goal: To help children learn about their own qualities, to help them maintain friendships.

Directions: 1. Ask children what they do to help make friendships, what a friend means to them, and any other comments about friendship. Write these on a large flip chart, board, or butcher paper.

2. Play the cassette/record.

3. Stress that friendships are important. People need to do their part in keeping friendships by listening, sharing, playing together, etc.

4. Give each child a pencil and the "Friends" handout. Let children try to work independently after the facilitator has gone over the activity instructions. The facilitator should go around to each child to help develop stories, spelling, wording, etc. For children who cannot write, use outline of friends page and have them draw pictures inside the outline.

5. After the front of the page is complete, give each child a magazine, scissors, and glue. Have them look for several small pictures of friends doing things together. Have them glue or tape these pictures to the back of the "Friends" handout page.

Discussion: Facilitator reads each child's story to the group (unless the child does not approve). Find something to praise the child about. Return handout page to each child and let children share their pictures on the back of the sheet.

HEALTHY SNACK TIME
(10 minutes)

Foods: Several flavors of granola bars (oat, chocolate chip)
Several types of juice (pineapple, orange, cranberry)

Directions: Cut granola bars into small slices. Allow children to taste all flavors. Do the same with juice. Let them judge which ones they like best individually and as a group.

Discussion: Talk about the four food groups, and where today's snack fits in the groups.

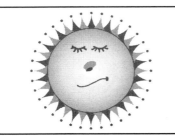

GOODBYE
(5 minutes)

Directions: Have all the children sit in a circle and tell the group something really special about a friend or family member. They can use their "Friends" handout to explain their feelings.

REMEMBER THE POSITIVE DAILY MESSAGE!

friends

I have many friends. Some of my friends are

_____

_____

_____

_____

My best friend is

_____

_____

Sometimes it is hard to make new friends.
Here is a story about making friends…

_____

_____

_____

_____

_____

_____

_____

_____

_____

_____

_____

Name:

_____

ACTIVITY PAGE

ACTIVITY 6

FAMILY AND FRIENDS

BEFORE THE SESSION

Materials:

• Paint, crayons, chalk, or colored pencils in the following colors: yellow, green, blue, black, red, purple, brown, orange, and gray

• Plain white paper

• *The Missing Piece Meets the Big O* by Shel Silverstein

Preparation Needed in Advance:

Prepare a large color chart with pictures to describe feelings. See p. 112 for directions.

HELLO
I'm a Good Friend
(5 minutes)

Facilitator: Introduce yourself and the *S.K.I.T.* program. Discuss the rules for being a part of the group. (Refer to Poster or Rules page.)

All children sit in a circle on the floor. Have each child tell why he/she thinks that he/she is a good friend to someone else (i.e., I think I am a good friend because I am always ready to listen to my friend's problems). After each child has answered, ask each child how he/she thinks he/she could be a better friend (i.e., I think I could be a better friend if I let John ride my bike sometimes). Talk about how families can be friends, too (i.e., My brother is my friend because he lets me borrow his favorite belt when I ask).

REMEMBER TO REINFORCE THE POSITIVE DAILY MESSAGE WITH EACH CHILD SOMETIME DURING THE SESSION.

"YOU ARE A SMART, FUN, CARING PERSON!"
"YES, I AM!"
"IF YOU DON'T FEEL LIKE YOU ARE, FAKE IT 'TIL YOU MAKE IT!"

S.K.I.T. LEARNING ACTIVITY
(30–35 minutes)

Color My Feeling

Goal: To enhance children's awareness of different feelings and how those feelings can affect how someone treats another person.

Make a color chart using pictures and colors to describe feelings. Mark the chart as follows:

RED	=	*ANGER*
PURPLE	=	*RAGE or* *OUT OF CONTROL*
BLUE	=	*SAD*
BLACK	=	*VERY SAD*
GREEN	=	*JEALOUS*
BROWN	=	*BORED*
GRAY	=	*LONESOME*
YELLOW	=	*HAPPY*
ORANGE	=	*EXCITEMENT*

Directions: 1. Discuss the color chart with the children. Be sure that they understand what each "feeling" word means by giving an example such as: "rage is stronger than anger because when you feel rage you may want to hurt someone" and "black is the color you see most often at funerals when someone dies."

2. Give each child two pieces of white paper. Tell them to fill the first sheet with feelings that **they** have had in their lives. (It will be helpful to offer an example of a Feeling Page.)

S.K.I.T.
LEARNING *(cont'd)*
ACTIVITY

3. Tell children to take the color that they feel most describes them, and paint or draw the size of that feeling on the sheet. Children can use designs such as squares, circles, or triangles, if they want to.

4. Now tell children to take the next "feeling" color that is in their lives. Children continue this until they have used either all the colors, or all of colors that they choose to use. The paper will be full of color or colors.

5. Tell the children to take the other white sheet of paper and do the same, except this time describing the **feelings** of a friend or a family member. Children do **not** have to name this person if they do not want to.

Discussion: After all drawings are completed, ask children what color they would color the page, if they could only use **one** color. Spend the rest of the time talking about how different feelings make you act differently toward other people, and make people act differently toward you.

READING/ RELAXATION
(15 minutes)

The Missing Piece Meets the Big O

Facilitator: Share the following book with the group. Have children participate by asking questions as the story progresses.

The Missing Piece Meets the Big 0 by Shel Silverstein

Discussion: Talk about the meaning of the story. Ask the children which part of the story they like the best.

HEALTHY SNACK TIME
(10 minutes)

Foods: Wheat crackers
Peanut butter
100% juice

Directions: As children eat, have each child say the following saying to the child next to him/her, continuing around the circle: "I like crackers, I like peanut butter. I like peanut butter and crackers. Do you?" After each child has said this alone, have them all say it together.

Discussion: Talk about the "hidden" fats in some foods, like peanut butter and crackers.

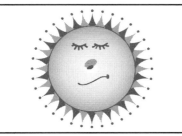

GOODBYE
(5 minutes)

Directions: Have each child pick out a color in the room that expresses his/her feeling **right now** (i.e., I see a yellow cup, I feel happy right now).

REMEMBER THE POSITIVE DAILY MESSAGE !

NOTES:

ACTIVITY 7
CHEMICAL DEPENDENCY

BEFORE THE SESSION	

Materials:

- Handout:
  The Bottle Barrier

- Construction paper
- Catalog or magazines
- Scissors
- Glue
- Colored paper
  (cut into strips)
- Markers
- Scotch tape

HELLO
My Favorite Games
(5 minutes)

Facilitator: Introduce yourself and the *S.K.I.T.* program. Discuss the rules for being a part of the group. (Refer to Poster or Rules page.)

Directions: Sitting Indian-style on the floor, have each child say his/her name and what his/her favorite thing or game to play is: what they enjoy playing or playing with the most.

Example: My name is Max, and I like to play "cowboy" best.

REMEMBER TO REINFORCE THE POSITIVE DAILY MESSAGE WITH EACH CHILD SOMETIME DURING THE SESSION.

"YOU ARE A SMART, FUN, CARING PERSON!"
"YES, I AM!"
"IF YOU DON'T FEEL LIKE YOU ARE, FAKE IT 'TIL YOU MAKE IT!"

GAME/ EXERCISE ACTIVITY
(10 minutes)

Fruit Basket Upset

Directions:　This is a circle game, similar to musical chairs. There is one less chair than people in the circle. (If there are no chairs in the room, use construction paper to mark spaces on the floor.) The facilitator calls out a statement to make children scramble. To make sure that the game is not competitive, have children who lose chairs/space state the directive to the remaining players, or make up their own directive.

Example:
- Everyone with jeans on: change chairs.
  TAKE OUT ANOTHER CHAIR OR SPACE

- Everyone who ate breakfast this morning: find a new chair.
  TAKE OUT ANOTHER CHAIR OR SPACE

- Everyone with blue eyes: scramble to a new chair.
  TAKE OUT ANOTHER CHAIR OR SPACE

- Everyone who likes to watch TV: scramble to a new chair.
  TAKE OUT ANOTHER CHAIR OR SPACE

Make up more directives, until there is only one chair/space left.

After the game is over, have children sit in a circle and tell how it felt when they did not have a space.

S.K.I.T. LEARNING ACTIVITY
(30–35 minutes)

The Bottle Barrier

Goal: To help show the hidden feelings of family members who are affected by alcohol or drug use. To help children process these feelings.

Directions: Before beginning with the pictures, facilitator should discuss the definition of substance abuse/chemical dependency. One that is commonly used is *The continued use of a substance which causes an individual to change behavior and affect the lives of others around him/her in a negative manner.*

1. Explain that when one member of a family abuses liquor or drugs, all family members are affected.

2. Each child is to cut from the magazine or catalog figures that represent members of a family. It can be their own family or a fictional one. Encourage children to talk about substance abuse they have seen in their family, on TV, etc. Do **not** ask direct personal questions.

3. Have children glue the pictures of their family to the construction paper.

4. Have children cut (or facilitator pre-cuts) the pictures of the bottle, pill, and crack jar, and glue one or all of these to the family pictures.

5. Using markers, have children write or draw on the strips of colored paper how family members or friends feel when someone they know abuses the substance (i.e., hurt, mad, sad, scared, stressful, etc.). Have children tape these strips to the picture.

Discussion: Ask each child to show his/her family picture and tell who the family members are in the picture. Have them read the different feelings written on the strips. (Once again, do not discourage a child's discussion of substance abuse within his/her family, but do **not** ask direct questions about his/her family situation.)

HEALTHY SNACK TIME
(10 minutes)

Foods: Pre-sliced/cut fruit pieces such as cherries, pineapple, peaches, apples, etc. If using canned products, use those packed in water, not syrup. Place each type in a separate container.
Coconut
Vanilla yogurt with a splash of cherry juice (optional)
Nuts
Paper cups and spoons
Water

Directions: Have each child **create** his/her own **fruit delight** by selecting items to put in the paper cup.

Discussion: Talk about the importance of eating fruits and veggies every day.

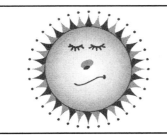

GOODBYE
(5 minutes)

Discussion: Have children sit in a circle and tell what they liked best about the session. All hold hands and squeeze while repeating the *POSITIVE DAILY MESSAGE.*

THE BOTTLE BARRIER

Pills

Crack

GIN

Alcohol

NOTES:

ACTIVITY 8
CHEMICAL DEPENDENCY

<table>
<tr><td>

BEFORE THE SESSION
....

Materials:

• Index cards (see below for preparation notes)

• White typing or drawing paper

• Crayons or colored pencils

Preparation Needed in Advance:
Prepare index cards with the questions on pp. 128–129.

</td><td>

HELLO
What Do I See?
(5 minutes)

Facilitator: Introduce yourself and the *S.K.I.T.* program. Discuss the rules for being a part of the group. (Refer to Poster or Rules page.)

Have children sit in a circle. Ask each child to tell the group an object that he/she **sees** in the room/space. After all have responded, ask the children, one at a time, to tell one thing that they like to **do**. After all have had the opportunity to speak, have each child tell how he/she **feels** today (i.e., I feel happy today, I feel sad today).

When all have finished, ask each child what they like to **talk** about the most. This **Hello** will serve as an introduction to the Seeing, Talking, Doing, and Feeling game that they are about to play.

REMEMBER TO REINFORCE THE POSITIVE DAILY MESSAGE WITH EACH CHILD SOMETIME DURING THE SESSION.

"YOU ARE A SMART, FUN, CARING PERSON!"
"YES, I AM!"
"IF YOU DON'T FEEL LIKE YOU ARE, FAKE IT 'TIL YOU MAKE IT!"

</td></tr>
</table>

S.K.I.T. LEARNING ACTIVITY
(30–35 minutes)

Seeing, Talking, Doing, and Feeling Game

Goal: To help children understand their feelings about substance abuse and process their previously suppressed or repressed thoughts, feelings, and actions.

Directions: 1. Facilitator or other person prepares the question cards **prior** to this session. These cards can be saved and used again.

2. Have children sit in a circle on the floor or around a table. Mix the cards together and place them in the middle of the circle.

3. Explain to the children that you will start the game. Each child will select a card from the stack and try to answer the question with the truth (i.e., Q: How do you feel right now? A: I am very sad today.). Help children who cannot read.

4. When the child finishes answering his/her question, the card is placed in another stack. Keep going around the circle until all cards are selected or children start to become fidgety. Do not force anyone to give an answer. Remember, children can pass their turn if they choose. Even if they do not respond **externally**, chances are they are responding **internally**.

5. Allow children to "free draw" immediately after this game for 5–10 minutes.

Discussion: Have each child discuss his/her drawing with the rest of the group.

READING/ RELAXATION
(15 minutes)

A Problem at Home

Facilitator: Show the children the following motion to express the above actions:

Seeing-	Blink eyes several times
Talking-	Move mouth up and down as if talking
Doing-	Clap hands or stomp feet
Feeling-	Make a face that expresses a particular feeling (i.e., happy—smile, sad—frown, angry—grit teeth, excited—mouth open wide, lonely—hands around waist, etc.)

Facilitator: Now read the following story to them aloud. Have them express the actions in the story with the above motions.

Story: A PROBLEM AT HOME

It was really early in the morning. Sally woke up and looked around to **see** if the sun was shining outside. She could hear her mother **talking** downstairs in a really loud voice. She was **feeling** really **sad** because her mother was screaming at her dad about his drinking too much beer.

Her mother kept **talking** to her dad, saying that she was **feeling** really **angry** that he was late last night and had been drinking too much.

Dad said that he was tired of hearing her **talk** and scream at him. Mom said that she thought he should go and **see** someone that could help him with his problem.

READING/ RELAXATION *(cont'd)*
(15 minutes)

Sally didn't know what to **do**. She was feeling very **lonely**.

Sally decided that she would call a number that the teacher gave her at school. The teacher told the class that this was a number they could call when they were **feeling angry, sad, lonely,** and needed someone to **talk** to.

Sally decided to **do** it. She picked up the phone and dialed the number. A really nice woman started **talking** to Sally about her problem. Sally also found out that there was a group that she could go to that would help her to **see** the problem better, help her **talk** about her mom and dad, and help her to **do** something about her **feelings**.

Discussion: Have children describe the group that Sally was going to attend.

(At this time the facilitator can give each child a card which gives a children's support group phone number to call if there is one in the area. If there is not one in the area, the facilitator can discuss other agencies or organizations that can help them.)

HEALTHY SNACK TIME
(10 minutes)

Foods: Different flavors of rice cakes
100% juice

Directions: Take a poll to see which flavor of rice cakes the children like best. (They usually choose the popcorn flavor.)

Discussion: Talk about ways to make a "junk food" snack healthy. *Example:* making popcorn in an air popper instead of using oil.

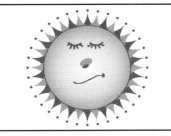

GOODBYE
(5 minutes)

Directions: Have children stand in a circle and close their eyes. Ask each child to tell what he/she **sees** with his/her eyes closed. Have all the children say the word **happy** at the same time. Tell them how good it is to hear them **talk**. Have children hold hands, and **talk** about how good it is to **feel** that person's hand (i.e., warm, soft). Ask them what they are going to **do** when they leave the session.

REMEMBER THE POSITIVE DAILY MESSAGE!

Cards for Seeing, Talking, Doing, and Feeling Game

SEEING Cards:

What do you see in the room that you really like?

What do you see in the room that you really do not like?

What do you see in the room that makes you very happy?

What do you see in the room that makes you very sad?

What do you see in the room that makes you very angry?

What do you see in the room that makes you very excited?

Have you ever seen anyone drunk or on drugs?

TALKING Cards:

What one thing do you really like to talk about with your family?

What one thing do you really like to talk about with your best friend?

What one thing do you NOT like to talk about with your family?

What one thing do you NOT like to talk about with your best friend?

What one thing does your mother or father (or whoever you live with) like to listen to you talk about?

What one thing would you like to talk about, but you do not feel like you can or should talk about?

What one thing would you like to talk with your parents about, but you are not sure they will listen?

If you had an imaginary friend, what would you talk about with him/her?

If someone you were really close to had too many drinks or too many drugs, what would you talk to them about?

If someone you were really close to had too many drinks or too many drugs, who would you talk to about it (i.e., that person, a friend, an imaginary friend)?

DOING Cards:

What one thing do you like to do best?

What one thing do you really not like to do?

What one thing do you do that you think you do very well?

What one thing do you do that you wish you could do better?

What one thing does your Dad, Mom, or whoever you live with do that you like?

What one thing does your Dad, Mom, or whoever you live with do that you do NOT like?

If you could do one thing, more than anything else, what would you do?

What do people who drink too much or use drugs too much do that really makes you mad?

What do people who drink too much or use drugs too much do that really makes you sad?

FEELING Cards:

How do you feel right now?

How do you feel when someone calls you a bad name?

How do you feel when someone tells you that you are really a great person?

How do you feel when someone tells you that you are ugly?

How do you (or would you) feel if someone is around that is drunk or using too many drugs?

How do you feel about people who drink too much or use too many drugs?

How do you feel when you do not keep a promise to someone?

How do you feel when someone else does not keep a promise to you?

NOTES:

AGES 9 THRU 12

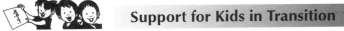

ACTIVITY 1

SELF-ESTEEM

BEFORE THE SESSION	
Materials:	

- Handouts:
  IALAC tags

- Tape
- Crayons
- Scissors
- 1-hole punch
- Yarn or string

Preparation Needed in Advance:
In addition to the handouts for the activity, use the IALAC handout to make an extra necklace for each of the children. These will be distributed at the end of the session.

HELLO
The Name Chain
(5 minutes)

Facilitator: Introduce yourself and the *S.K.I.T.* program. Discuss the rules for being a part of the group. (Refer to Poster or Rules page.)

Have all the children sit in a circle. Have someone start by saying his/her name. The next child says the name of the first person and his/her own name. The last person must say the names of all the other children in the group. If he/she accomplishes this, he/she can choose anyone in the room to do the same thing. If the one selected says all names correctly, he/she can choose anyone to do the task…and so on.

REMEMBER TO REINFORCE THE POSITIVE DAILY MESSAGE WITH EACH CHILD SOMETIME DURING THE SESSION.

"YOU ARE A SMART, FUN, CARING PERSON!"
"YES, I AM!"
"IF YOU DON'T FEEL LIKE YOU ARE, FAKE IT 'TIL YOU MAKE IT!"

GAME/ EXERCISE ACTIVITY
(10 minutes)

Rag Doll Dance
(Less than 5 children)

Directions: Play a record or tape of rock-and-roll or disco music. Begin by taking a few deep breaths, then shake each arm and leg for 8 counts each, making the motions like a rag doll. Then, shake the right arm and leg together, then left arm and leg. Bend over and shake the upper part of the torso, arms hanging down. Have children create different combinations of body parts to shake with the music.

Shoe Factory
(5 or more children)

Directions: Begin by sitting in a circle. Have everyone remove their shoes and throw them in the center, like a ceremonial pile. Next, each person (one at a time) goes to the pile and selects an unmatched pair of shoes, neither of which is his/her own shoe, and puts them on (if the shoe is too small, just put the toes inside).

Everyone chants, **"Shoe! Shoe! Shoe!"** and shuffles around trying to find the people who are wearing the mates to the shoes they are wearing. When a matching shoe is found, keep the matching feet together so that all the shoes are in proper pairs. This should create an interesting configuration of feet.

"But Where Are My Shoes?" the facilitator asks. All in the group should then remove their shoes in place, which should leave all shoes matched. Group again yells, **"Shoes! Shoes! Shoes! Where are my shoes?"** Children go to their **own** pair of shoes and put them on again.

134

S.K.I.T. LEARNING ACTIVITY
(30–35 minutes)

IALAC—<u>I</u> <u>A</u>m <u>L</u>ovable <u>A</u>nd <u>C</u>apable

Goal: To help children recognize that things that happen can make them feel **more** or **less** lovable and capable. To help children identify how they can help themselves and others feel **more** rather than less lovable and capable.

Directions: 1. Distribute IALAC sheet to each child. Ask children to do the following:
   A. Color in the letters.
   B. Cut out the IALAC sign.
   C. Punch a hole where indicated and pull yarn or string through the hole and tie it.
   D. All children can now wear this sign as a necklace. (It will help to show them a finished example.)

2. Encourage children to guess what the letters stand for.

3. Before reading the following story, instruct children to do the following:
   A. If something bad happens in the story to the boy, the children should tear off a part of their sign.
   B. Facilitator can use the "thumbs down" motion while telling the story to indicate that children should tear off a part of their IALAC sign.
4. Read the IALAC story on the next page.

S.K.I.T. LEARNING ACTIVITY *(cont'd)*

IALAC

Think of the boy who gets up in the morning with a big IALAC sign showing right straight across his chest. The first voice he hears is his father saying, "Get out of bed, lazy bones, or you'll never amount to anything." He goes on, "Did you get your homework done last night? If you would only plan your time better and study more, you would be as good as your sister."

The boy gets out of bed, looks for his homework, finds it rumpled on the floor. He looks for his shoes and cannot find them. His mother calls for him to hurry. He has to put on some old worn-out tennis shoes with no shoelaces. He hurries down to breakfast. "What's for breakfast, Mom?" She says, "You don't have time for anything but cereal. You're going to miss the bus as it is." He gulps down the cereal and runs down the street to the bus stop.

The boy joins the other children waiting for the bus. One of the boys comes up behind him and knocks the books out of his hands. His homework, already rumpled, now ends up in a mud puddle. Quickly, he gathers up his papers and books, gets on the bus and sits all alone, as the other children have all found someone else to sit with.

In school, the teacher announces that there will be a spelling test. The boy feels okay about this, because he did study spelling the night before, but he can't find his pencil—it must have dropped at the bus stop. He turns to the girl next and says, "Bring your own pencils to school. I'm not giving you mine." The teacher is very mad that he does not have his pencil, and hands him one with a frown.

S.K.I.T. LEARNING ACTIVITY *(cont'd)*

Later on when the children line up for recess, the teacher says, "I like the way the girls are lining up." On the playground, two boys have been selected to choose up sides for a kick-ball game. The boy waits to be chosen, but when everyone else is on a team, one of the boys says, "You take him, we don't want him. He can't kick very well, or even catch."

During the lunch, the boy is carefully carrying his tray to the table when he trips and the tray goes everywhere. Everyone laughs. After school, when the boy gets home, he calls out, "Mom, how about some milk and cookies?" But Mom isn't home. She had an appointment. He goes in to watch his favorite TV show, settles down on the couch, and his big brother comes in and changes the TV station.

At supper, when everyone is eating and talking about the events of the day, he tries to get in a word about what happened to him during the day, but it seems that what everyone else has to say is more important and no one listens. By the time he gets ready for bed, the only thing remaining of his IALAC sign is a tiny piece just about big enough to cover a button on his pajamas.

The next morning when he wakes up, his new IALAC sign is smaller than the one he had on yesterday. Will it get torn away again?

S.K.I.T.
LEARNING   *(cont'd)*
ACTIVITY

Discussion: Ask the following questions:

1. What does IALAC stand for? *I Am Lovable And Capable.*

2. What were some of the good things that happened to the boy?

3. What were some of the bad things that happened to the boy?

4. What did the boy's IALAC sign look like at the end of the day?

5. If you were the boy, how would you feel?

6. What were some of the put-downs that the boy had during the day?

7. What kind of put-downs have you had to live through in the past week?

8. What can you do so that you don't feel bad when you are faced with put-downs?

9. What can you do so that other people feel good about themselves?

10. Repeat: **I Am Lovable And Capable.**

11. Go around the room and ask each child why he/she thinks that he/she is **Lovable and Capable.**

HEALTHY SNACK TIME
(10 minutes)

Foods: Presliced/cut fruit pieces (cherries, pineapple, peaches, apples, etc.). If using canned products, use those packed in water, not in syrup. Place each type in a separate container.
Coconut
Vanilla yogurt with a splash of cherry juice
Nuts
Paper cups and spoons
Water

Discussion: Talk about ways to make a "junk food" snack healthy. *Example:* making popcorn in an air popper instead of using oil.

GOODBYE
(5 minutes)

Directions: Have each child repeat, **I Am Lovable And Capable** five times. Let children whisper this statement five times. Let them laugh while saying it five times. Let them jump up and down while saying it five times. Have them chant this saying as they go out the door. Give each child a new IALAC sign.

REMEMBER THE POSITIVE DAILY MESSAGE!

IALAC

Put yarn here

ACTIVITY 2
SELF-ESTEEM

BEFORE THE SESSION

Materials:

- Plain white typing paper
- Construction paper
- 1-hole punch
- Large tapestry needle (optional)
- Yarn
- Magazines
- Scissors, glue, ruler
- Pencils or pens
- *The Velveteen Rabbit* by Margery Williams

HELLO
My Best Quality
(5 minutes)

Facilitator: Introduce yourself and the *S.K.I.T.* program. Discuss the rules for being a part of the group. (Refer to Poster or Rules page.)

Everyone sits in a circle at the table or on the floor. Each child says his/her name and describes his/her best quality and why.

Example: My name is Linda and I think that my honesty is my best quality because I want people to know that I tell the truth.

REMEMBER TO REINFORCE THE POSITIVE DAILY MESSAGE WITH EACH CHILD SOMETIME DURING THE SESSION.

"YOU ARE A SMART, FUN, CARING PERSON!"
"YES, I AM!"
"IF YOU DON'T FEEL LIKE YOU ARE, FAKE IT 'TIL YOU MAKE IT!"

S.K.I.T. LEARNING ACTIVITY
(30–35 minutes)

The Journal

Goal: To encourage the practice of writing down thoughts and feelings in order to better understand and appreciate the self.

Directions:

1. Take four sheets of typing paper, fold in half. Fold a sheet of construction paper in half.

2. Open the construction paper and typing paper and lay sheets of typing paper on top of the construction paper, 2 inches from the top and bottom.

3. Cut a length of yarn about 24" long and thread through the tapestry needle. Starting at the outside of the book, pass the needle through all five sheets of paper to the inside, then back to the outside. Tie the yarn in a bow on the outside to look like a book.

4. Have children cut a picture or pictures for the cover and print their names and then the word "Journal" (i.e., Tommy's Journal).

5. Have children write a feeling message on the inside of the cover such as *"My Private Thoughts"* or *"This is My Feelings Book."*

Discussion: Tell them that each day they can write a message in their book that expresses how they feel that day. It can be one word or many words, or it can be a picture or many pictures. After the book is filled, tell the children that they can begin another book, or just look back on this book and see how they felt during the days that they completed it. Stress that it is a private book, for no one else to see unless they want to show it to someone.

READING/ RELAXATION
(15 minutes)

The Velveteen Rabbit

Directions: Have all the children sit Indian-style on the floor. Instruct them to roll their necks to the left very slowly in a complete circle. Then, have them roll their necks to the right very slowly in the same manner. Tell them that you are going to tell them a story about being **real**. Ask the group what they think being **real** is. How do you get to be real?

Have children rest in a comfortable position, either lying down or sitting.

Facilitator: Read the story *The Velveteen Rabbit,* by Margery Williams.

Discussion: Talk about the book with the children, making sure that each has the opportunity to tell how he/she liked or disliked the story.

HEALTHY SNACK TIME
(10 minutes)

Foods: Cereal that has holes (Cheerios, Apple Jacks, Fruit Loops) or other types that will string
Dried fruit, fruit roll-ups or pieces
Yarn
Milk or water to drink

Directions: Have the children string cereal necklaces, and then have fun eating them!

Discussion: Talk about the everyday foods that are good sources of vitamins and minerals.

Example: Milk has vitamin D and calcium. Raisins have lots of iron. Ask the kids if they can name any other good sources.

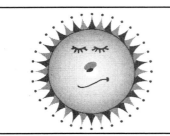

GOODBYE
(5 minutes)

Directions: Have all the children sit Indian-style on the floor. Have each one tell what he/she liked about the session and one thing that each learned about himself/herself.

REMEMBER THE POSITIVE DAILY MESSAGE!

ACTIVITY 3

DECISION-MAKING

BEFORE THE SESSION	

Materials:

- Poster boards (3 or 4)
- Magazines
- Scissors
- Glue

HELLO
The Giant Birthday Party
(5 minutes)

Facilitator: Introduce yourself and the *S.K.I.T.* program. Discuss the rules for being a part of the group. (Refer to Poster or Rules page.)

Have children sit in a circle. Tell them to imagine that this is a giant birthday party. "You know all the people here, but nobody else knows anybody at all. So of course you want us all to meet each other.

"Your job in the next 3 minutes is to introduce everybody here to everybody else here. Don't introduce yourself to anybody, just go up to someone like this and say 'Hi, what's your name?' ('Paula') 'Hi, Paula. Come with me and I will introduce you to someone else.' 'Hi, what's your name?' ('Jim') You say, 'Paula this is Jim, Jim this is Paula.' Now that you have introduced Paula to Jim, go and find someone else to meet and introduce.

"Of course, someone will come up to you and introduce you to someone else, too! We will time the activity, so you have 3 minutes. See if you can learn everyone's name."

HELLO   *(cont'd)*

Demonstrate and help the children get started. After everyone has finished, go around the circle and see who can remember all of the names.

REMEMBER TO REINFORCE THE POSITIVE DAILY MESSAGE WITH EACH CHILD SOMETIME DURING THE SESSION.

"YOU ARE A SMART, FUN, CARING PERSON!"
"YES, I AM!"
"IF YOU DON'T FEEL LIKE YOU ARE,
FAKE IT 'TIL YOU MAKE IT!"

GAME/ EXERCISE ACTIVITY
(10 minutes)

Simultaneous Songs

Facilitator: Give children the following instructions:
"Everyone gets a chance to listen to people singing songs on the radio, and lots of us get the chance to sing songs ourselves. Whether it's singing together with a group of people, or just singing in the shower, it can be fun to sing. Sometimes we even make up our own words or compose a song. It's really fun to sing a song that you have written yourself. It can be sad, happy, silly, etc."

GAME/ EXERCISE ACTIVITY *(cont'd)*

"This game is called *Simultaneous Songs*—how many know what that means?

"We are all going to compose our own songs and sing them at the same time! However, if we're all singing different songs at the same time, they all need to have the same tune so it's not total chaos. Let's agree on a familiar tune that we can all sing. Who's got one?"

Example: Row, Row, Row Your Boat.

"Let's all hum the tune a couple of times. This is going to be a song in five different verses. Anyone can call out the topic."

Example: Desserts.

"Now we will all sing our own song about Desserts to the tune of Row, Row, Row Your Boat. 1-2-3…**SING!**"

Example: "John sings: I like frozen yogurt very very much…" Heather sings: "Chocolate ice cream is my favorite, every single day…"

As soon as everyone has sung through their song one or two times, someone else calls out the category for the next verse.

Example: Friends.

Follow the same procedure. The fifth verse/category is the finale. Each child can sing one of the songs from **any** of the four verses (desserts, friends, etc.) at the same time or sing **all** verses.

S.K.I.T. LEARNING ACTIVITY
(30–35 minutes)

Another Kind of Ad

Goal: To help children recognize how advertising can influence the decisions that we make.

Directions:
1. Divide the children into pairs or threesomes (if there are not very many children, they can work on the project alone or as one group).

2. Instruct children to pretend that they are directors of an advertising company. The president of this company has decided to produce ads which will influence 9–12-year-olds about something.

Example: Cigarette smoking.

3. Tell the children, "You are the directors, so get started!" Give each group/child a poster board. Instruct them to use half for the **for** ad and half for the **against** ad.

Example: One side encourages you to smoke, the other side does not.

Discussion: When children are finished, have each group show and explain their ad. Talk about how TV, radio, and magazines influence our choices. Talk about how we can make our **own** decisions. Tape posters on the wall.

HEALTHY SNACK TIME
(10 minutes)

Foods: Rice cakes (plain)
Peanut butter
100% juice (3 flavors)

Take a juice poll and see which one wins as favorite.

Discussion: Talk about the "hidden" fats in some foods, like peanut butter and crackers.

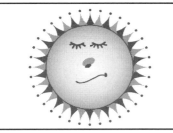

GOODBYE
(5 minutes)

Directions: Stand in a circle holding hands, and have everyone close their eyes and repeat:

"I am loved exactly the way I am today. The only thing that I can change in the world is how I look and feel about me and other people. I can make decisions on how I feel about myself and others. I can like myself just like I am."

REMEMBER THE POSITIVE DAILY MESSAGE!

NOTES:

ACTIVITY 4

DECISION-MAKING

BEFORE THE SESSION	

Materials:

- Index cards
- Chalkboard or large poster paper
- Scissors, magazines, glue sticks
- Tape of ocean music, or another relaxation tape such as New Age music (i.e., George Winston tapes)

HELLO
First Name, Last Name
(5 minutes)

Facilitator: Introduce yourself and the *S.K.I.T.* program. Discuss the rules for being a part of the group. (Refer to Poster or Rules page.)

Note: Index cards are needed for this activity.

Directions: Have all children sit in a circle on the floor. Ask each one's name. Have them write their first names on an index card, and throw the cards in the middle of the circle, names not showing. Have children select a card from the stack and point to the person with that first name. Have children write down their last names on the back of the card with their first name. Don't let anyone see! Throw the cards in the middle of the circle, with the first names up and last names down. Have children draw cards and connect last names with the children. Have children turn over the cards to check the first names.

REMEMBER TO REINFORCE THE POSITIVE DAILY MESSAGE WITH EACH CHILD SOMETIME DURING THE SESSION.

HELLO (cont'd)

*"YOU ARE A SMART, FUN,
CARING PERSON!"
"YES, I AM!"
"IF YOU DON'T FEEL LIKE YOU ARE,
FAKE IT 'TIL YOU MAKE IT!"*

S.K.I.T. LEARNING ACTIVITY
(30–35 minutes)

You Can Make Your Own Decisions

Goal: To help youth become aware of "other things to do" as alternatives to counter-productive behavior and dealing with peer pressure.

Directions: 1. Ask the group about some of the things that people do at school that are against the rules or not acceptable.

Example: Fighting.

2. Make a list of these behaviors on the chalkboard or poster board.

3. After a list has been established, have the children put them in order of the most unacceptable to the most acceptable.

S.K.I.T.
LEARNING *(cont'd)*
ACTIVITY

---

4. Generate another list of positive alternatives to these activities.

Example: Sports, video games, etc.

5. Write these ideas on the poster board.

6. Ask this question for problem solving among the group: What can you say to a friend who has just asked you to meet him after school to fight with two guys from another school? (Question can be different, depending on the list established from #1.)

7. Brainstorm with the group.

8. Now, talk about what in the past has made them feel good.

Example: Taking a long walk or riding a dirt bike.

9. Divide the group into pairs or threesomes, and give each group a poster board. Have them create a collage of positive alternatives.

Discussion: Have youth discuss their pictures with the group. These posters should be placed on the wall next to the posters created in Activity 3, if that activity was completed recently.

READING/
RELAXATION
(15 minutes)

Floating on the Ocean

Facilitator: You will need a tape of ocean music, or another relaxation tape such as New Age music (i.e., George Winston tapes).

Begin playing the music very softly.

Directions: Get together in a group of three (or groups of three if there are many) and decide which of you is going to be a submarine, a sailboat, and an ocean liner.

"We are going to do a group relaxation fantasy together about floating in the middle of the ocean. The Submarines are going to get relaxed first, and the two partners will assist, then we will rotate. So Submarines, the first thing you will do is stand with your feet together and your hands hanging loosely at your sides. Take a deep breath and hold it, and as you exhale let your eyes close and let your body relax. Imagine yourself floating in the middle of the ocean. Imagine that you are hearing waves breaking on the shore. Listen to those waves, and feel yourself floating on the ocean, totally safe, totally taken care of.

"Sailboats and Ocean liners, stand directly behind the Submarine now and put one hand on his/her shoulder and one hand on the small of his/her back (demonstrate). Begin rocking the weight very gently now, back on the heels, then forward to standing balance again, then to the front on the toes, rocking him/her back and forth in time to the waves and music. Now, slowly stop this motion, and Submarine, you may now open your eyes and come back to the room and thank your partners for the gift."

Have each group do the same for the Ocean liners and the Sailboats.

Discussion: Have youth talk about their feelings during the activity. What do they think was the gift?

HEALTHY SNACK TIME
(10 minutes)

Foods: Frozen yogurt
Paper plates
Squeezable cake decorator frosting
Water (to drink)

Directions: Have each child decorate his/her plate with the decorator frosting. (We know this isn't too healthy, but sometimes you just have to have fun!)

Have them dip the yogurt onto their plate. They can also decorate the frozen yogurt.

Discussion: Talk about the importance of drinking lots of water every day.

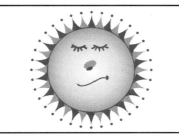

GOODBYE
(5 minutes)

Directions: Children are standing in a circle and holding hands. The facilitator gently squeezes the child's hand to the right of him/her. Each person squeezes the hand of the next person until it returns to the Facilitator.

While holding hands, repeat the *POSITIVE DAILY MESSAGE.*

NOTES:

ACTIVITY 5
FAMILY AND FRIENDS

BEFORE THE SESSION	**HELLO**

Materials:

- 8 ½ by 11 sheets of white poster board
- White paper plates with a border
- Colored marking pens or crayons, including red
- Glue sticks or glue
- Magazines
- Scissors

HELLO
Going on a Camping Trip
(5 minutes)

Facilitator: Introduce yourself and the *S.K.I.T.* program. Discuss the rules for being a part of the group. (Refer to Poster or Rules page.)

Directions: Have all children sit in a circle. Tell them that they are going on a camping trip and are taking two things that start with the same letter as their first name.

Example: My name is Mary and I am taking a Mat and a cup of Milk.

The second person does the same except he/she must include the last person's camping items. Continue until the entire group has had a turn. If the group is small, go around twice.

REMEMBER TO REINFORCE THE POSITIVE DAILY MESSAGE WITH EACH CHILD SOMETIME DURING THE SESSION.

"YOU ARE A SMART, FUN, CARING PERSON!"
"YES, I AM!"
"IF YOU DON'T FEEL LIKE YOU ARE, FAKE IT 'TIL YOU MAKE IT!"

157

GAME/ EXERCISE ACTIVITY
(15 minutes)

Train Station

Directions: Tell the children, "Pick a partner. Stand about 20 feet away from that person, but close enough that you can still maintain eye contact. Give that partner a little wave, so you can make sure that he/she sees you. Imagine that your partner is your best friend in the world—from the time you were both 4 years old. You haven't seen the person since then, but you just got a telegram saying, 'Meet me at the train station!' So…here you are at the train station, the train has just come in, and you are **very excited**! This is your best friend in the whole world. Now, one thing you have to know is that this whole thing takes place in slow motion."

Have children listen and begin to act out the scene. Say:

"You are going to move towards your partner **very slowly**, waving to him/her, maybe you're blowing kisses to him/her, very excited to see that person, ready to embrace him/her. All in slow motion.…As soon as you get about 2 feet away, you realize it is the **wrong person**! Needless to say, you are **upset**! You are very embarrassed, so what you do is pretend that all along you've been waving at someone behind him/her. You keep on going past your partner, moving slowly towards somebody else in the room."

Facilitator should repeat the above scenario until children have had the opportunity to encounter everyone in the room.

Discussion: Talk to children about how it made them feel to not know the person, be embarrassed, etc.

S.K.I.T. LEARNING ACTIVITY
(30–35 minutes)

Family Circles

Goal: To help children see how they relate to family members and friends.

Directions: 1. Give each child a poster board sheet. Have them glue the paper plate on the sheet, wherever they choose to position it. This paper plate represents their family circle.

2. Ask them to look through magazines and find a picture that best represents themselves and cut it out, placing it somewhere that they think they fit in the family. Explain that they may see themselves in the middle of the circle, to the side, on the edge, or outside the circle: any place that they feel they **fit** in the family.

3. Now have them look for pictures that represent other family members. They can define their family however they choose. The family may include friends, distant relatives, etc.

4. Have them glue these "family" members onto the picture, wherever they see them fitting.

Discussion: Talk about the pictures when they are completed.

Now have each child take a red marker and put an X on the place in the picture that they would like to be, if they are unhappy with where they are now. Have those who placed an X tell why they would like to be somewhere else in their family circle.

HEALTHY SNACK TIME
(10 minutes)

Foods: Several flavors of granola bars cut into small pieces (oat, chocolate chip, raisin, etc.)
100% juice

Directions: Put pieces on plates, and label them only with numbers: #1, #2, #3, etc. Have children test each flavor and vote on which flavor they like best. Let them judge which ones they like best individually and as a group. Reveal the flavor names after the vote.

Discussion: Talk about the four food groups, and where today's snack fits in the groups.

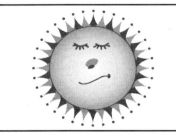

GOODBYE
(5 minutes)

Directions: Have all the children sit in a circle. Each person says goodbye to all of the others, until everyone has had the opportunity to talk.

All stand up, clasp hands, and in unison repeat the *POSITIVE DAILY MESSAGE.*

ACTIVITY 6

FAMILY AND FRIENDS

BEFORE THE SESSION	

Materials:

- Large sheet of paper or chalkboard
- Pens or chalk

HELLO
Where I'm From
(5 minutes)

Facilitator: Introduce yourself and the *S.K.I.T.* program. Discuss the rules for being a part of the group. (Refer to Poster or Rules page.)

Directions: Have all children sit in a circle. Have each state his/her name, what town they were born in (or if they don't know, what town they lived in recently). Have children discuss where their family members live right now.

REMEMBER TO REINFORCE THE POSITIVE DAILY MESSAGE WITH EACH CHILD SOMETIME DURING THE SESSION.

"YOU ARE A SMART, FUN, CARING PERSON!"
"YES, I AM!"
"IF YOU DON'T FEEL LIKE YOU ARE, FAKE IT 'TIL YOU MAKE IT!"

S.K.I.T. LEARNING ACTIVITY
(30 minutes)

Rules of the House

Goal: To help children understand feelings of others in the family and their own feelings about rules.

Directions:

1. Divide the children into two equal groups (or close to it). Appoint one group as the "Enforcers" and the other as the "Slaves." The Enforcers are the parents, since they make the rules and enforce them. The Slaves are you, the children in the family.

2. On the blackboard (or paper) write:
   Rules of the House

3. Give the group 10 minutes to name rules that their parents have for them. All may answer.

4. Now write on the board/paper:
   How I Will Enforce the Rules

5. Give the Enforcers 5 minutes to list how they will make sure that the above rules are followed.

6. Now write on the board/paper:
   How I Feel when I Have to Follow the Rules

7. Give the Slaves 5 minutes to list how they feel about the rules and the way they are going to be enforced.

S.K.I.T. LEARNING ACTIVITY *(cont'd)*

Discussion: Ask all children what kind of way works best to get them to follow rules that their parents set.

Example: When my mom asks me in a nice way to clean my room, I usually do it.

Reverse the roles, make the enforcers the slaves and vice versa, if there is time.

READING/ RELAXATION
(10 minutes)

Imagination Time

Facilitator: Have the group lay on the floor anywhere.

Directions: Tell the group to close their eyes and think of one family member. Picture him/her physically and how he/she acts. Think of all the good and bad qualities he/she has. Give children examples so they will be able to form a picture.

Now imagine this family member floating in the air above you. Suddenly, he/she comes down and enters your body. Think of how you feel being that person. Think of your good feelings and bad feelings. Try to feel and think like that family member feels and thinks.

Discussion: Have the group open their eyes and discuss how they felt being that other family member. Do the same thing again, but use a friend this time.

HEALTHY SNACK TIME
(10 minutes)

Foods: American, Swiss, and cheddar cheese slices
Crackers
Water or 100% juice

Directions: Do a taste test with the cheese. Have the children pick their favorite, with or without the crackers.

Discussion: Talk about the importance of moderation in eating some good foods.

Example: Cheese has protein (good), but it also has fat (bad).

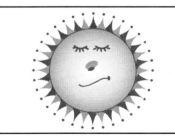

GOODBYE
(5 minutes)

Directions: Have children form two circles, one on the inside and one on the outside. (If there are only a few children, use another goodbye from the book.)

Have children on the inside face children on the outside and have each pair tell one another what they like. Children on the inside move around clockwise until all children have spoken to each other.

REMEMBER THE POSITIVE DAILY MESSAGE!

164

ACTIVITY 7
CHEMICAL DEPENDENCY

BEFORE THE SESSION	

Materials:

- New contemporary magazines
- Pens
- Writing paper

HELLO
Definitions
(5 minutes)

Facilitator: Introduce yourself and the *S.K.I.T.* program. Discuss the rules for being a part of the group. (Refer to Poster or Rules page.)

Directions: Have all children sit in a circle and ask them to define Chemical Dependency. First, have them introduce themselves and then give a definition. As a group, come up with one definition that everyone can agree on.

REMEMBER TO REINFORCE THE POSITIVE DAILY MESSAGE WITH EACH CHILD SOMETIME DURING THE SESSION.

"YOU ARE A SMART, FUN, CARING PERSON!"
"YES, I AM!"
"IF YOU DON'T FEEL LIKE YOU ARE, FAKE IT 'TIL YOU MAKE IT!"

GAME/ EXERCISE ACTIVITY
(15 minutes)

Argument

Directions: Have youth pick a partner. Facilitator says the following: "Let's go through the rules together. Decide who is going to go first. I will use myself as an example. Whatever I say, you say the opposite.

Example: I say, "**stop!**" You say, "**go!**" I say, "It's **cold.**" You say, "It's **hot.**"

"Make sure to say it clearly and loudly, but not screaming. When you play this game with your partners, start by speaking softly, get louder, then bring it back to soft again. The only other rule is that you cannot use the words 'I' or 'You.' The other member must speak at whatever level his partner is speaking at. Try hand motions and facial expressions to go along with what you are saying."

LET'S ARGUE!

Discussion: Ask group the following types of questions:

1. Did you feel comfortable arguing back and forth?

2. Did you like it better when the other person spoke softly or loudly?

3. Why?

4. How can we stop arguments from happening?

5. If we feel we need to argue, what are some rules we might make so that it doesn't turn into a fight?

S.K.I.T. LEARNING ACTIVITY
(30–35 minutes)

Media Search

Goal: To show youth how social pressures can have a major impact on us and possible substance abuse.

Directions: 1. Divide youth into two to three groups. Pass out one magazine to each group. Try to use ones that have not been cut or had pages torn out.

2. Have each group look through the magazines and count the number of ads that are trying to sell alcohol.

3. Have one person in each group write down the professions of the people that are in the alcohol ads (i.e., doctor, lawyer). If it is not stated in the ad, have them judge by the appearance and/or clothing.

4. Have all groups discuss the results.

5. Have each group go back through the magazines and count the number of ads that influence people **not** to use alcohol or drugs (articles may also be used).

6. Talk about the results.

7. Now have each group come up with a short television spot that tries to convince the others in the session not to use drugs/alcohol. Tell them that they can use the magazine ads to help.

8. Give each group time to perform their *S.K.I.T.*

Discussion: Talk about the impact of social pressures and how to recognize when someone is trying to influence you. Ask the children what strategies they learned from this activity that will help them resist the pressure to drink or do drugs.

HEALTHY SNACK TIME
(10 minutes)

Foods: Vegetable platter (carrots, celery, broccoli, etc.)
Ranch-style dip
Juice or water

Have children help prepare the tray, dividing up the responsibilities. Talk about the importance of eating fruits and vegetables every day. Take a poll on which veggies the group likes best, with or without dip.

Discussion: Talk about the importance of eating fruits and veggies every day.

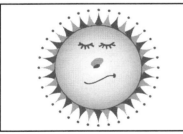

GOODBYE
(5 minutes)

Directions: Have each child tell what they did and didn't like about this session. Ask each child how they feel about alcohol and drugs.

REMEMBER THE POSITIVE DAILY MESSAGE!

ACTIVITY 8
CHEMICAL DEPENDENCY

BEFORE THE SESSION	

Materials:

- Handout:
  Feelings Wheel

- Several colors of yarn tied together and wound into a large ball

- Pens, pencils

HELLO
Energy Partners
(5 minutes)

Facilitator: Introduce yourself and the *S.K.I.T.* program. Discuss the rules for being a part of the group. (Refer to Poster or Rules page.)

Directions: Have children form into pairs and face their partner at arms length. Tell them to touch palms and close their eyes for about 30 seconds. Instruct them to feel the energy they are creating together. Now have them keep their eyes closed, but drop hands and both turn around three times without opening their eyes. They are to try and relocate their "energy partners" by touching palms again. After they have located palms, then tell them to open their eyes and introduce themselves to each other saying, "Hi, I am _____. We have just shared enough energy to _____."

Example: "Hi, I am Sandra. We have just shared enough energy to start a fire."

Ask children to find a new "energy partner" and go through the same exercise.

HELLO *(cont'd)*

REMEMBER TO REINFORCE THE POSITIVE DAILY MESSAGE
WITH EACH CHILD SOMETIME DURING THE SESSION.

"YOU ARE A SMART, FUN, CARING PERSON!"
"YES, I AM!"
*"IF YOU DON'T FEEL LIKE YOU ARE,
FAKE IT 'TIL YOU MAKE IT!"*

S.K.I.T. LEARNING ACTIVITY
(30–35 minutes)

Yarn Connections

Goal: To show that we are all interconnected, particularly in a family situation, and that what one person does affects all of the other members.

Directions:

1. Have children form a circle, and hand one person the ball of yarn.

2. Have them hold on to the end of the yarn and throw the ball to another person. That person catches the ball and holds on to the yarn by wrapping it around his/her hands, feet, waist, or whatever he/she chooses.

3. When all the yarn is gone, it will appear that the group is in a tangled mess.

S.K.I.T. LEARNING ACTIVITY *(cont'd)*

4. Have one person walk away from the group, still holding on to his/her yarn, and see what happens.

5. Talk to the group about their choices at this point in order to "get away" from the group. Let them either untangle themselves or cut the yarn, or act out another alternative that they have chosen.

Discussion: Point out that we do not live our lives in isolation, that what we do affects the lives of others around us. Talk about a mobile and how when one of the objects is removed, the rest of the mobile becomes unbalanced. Ask the following questions:

1. What happens when one member of the family is a substance abuser? (You may have to go over a definition of chemical dependency/substance abuse.)

2. What choices does the family have when one member continues to use drugs or alcohol? (*Example:* stay and accept, leave, become addicted.)

3. How does the rest of the family feel when one member is always drunk or high on drugs?

Facilitator: At this point you should relate substance abuse and chemical dependency to the yarn exercise.

READING/ RELAXATION
(15–20 minutes)

Clay Dough

Facilitator: Pass out "Feeling Wheel" handout and a pen or pencil to each group member.

Directions: Tell the children, "This is a Feeling Wheel. It's a tool that can help you focus on your feelings. At each of the four spokes of the wheel, write down a feeling that you are having. Take a couple of minutes to do this without talking to anyone else.

"Now, flip a coin in your mind." Give the group a few seconds to choose and then say, "If it came up heads, find one other person that is taller than you. If it came up tails, find someone shorter than you. Get together with your partner and figure out which one of you is A and which one is B. Those who are A's, raise your left hand. Those who are B's, raise your right hand.

"Now we are going to do some **sculpting**. For the first round, each A will pretend that he/she is clay or dough. Practice. Each B will pretend that he/she is the Sculptor or Artist. Practice.

"A will now whisper in B's ear one of the feelings that he/she placed on the wheel. B, you have 2 minutes to 'sculpt' or turn A into that feeling. Be an artist and create the feeling. A, you need to make sure that you let B change the shape of your body and facial features in order to create that feeling." (Facilitator may want to act as an example first.)

READING/ RELAXATION *(cont'd)*

After all artists are finished, the group will try to figure out what the feeling is that each artist has sculpted. Change roles, if there is time. Now have one artist (B) and one clay (A) come to the center of a circle, with all of the others sitting Indian-style.

Facilitator: "Artist, you will now sculpt a person who is an alcoholic or drug addict. Make the clay look like how that person feels." Have another child come to the center of the room, and have the artist sculpt how a family member of an alcoholic or drug addict feels. Continue by adding people to the center of the room until all children except the artist have been sculpted. Have the children look around at the expressions and motions of the others.

Discussion: Discuss the results.

HEALTHY SNACK TIME
(10 minutes)

Foods: English muffins or mini-bagels
Cream cheese (flavored with pineapple, strawberries)
100% juice

Directions: Take a poll to see which flavor of cream cheese the group likes best, on an English muffin or bagel.

Discussion: Talk about the difference between 10% and 100% juice, in terms of taste and nutritional value.

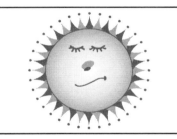

GOODBYE
(5 minutes)

Directions: Have all children return to a circle, standing and holding hands. Have each child tell what he/she liked best about today and how he/she feels right now.

REMEMBER THE POSITIVE DAILY MESSAGE!